GOOD & PROPER TEA

Happy brewing!

Emilie

GOOD & PROPER TEA

From leaf to cup, how to choose, brew and cook with tea

Emilie Holmes

Photography by Steven Joyce

Kyle Books

To our wonderful customers around the world
for allowing us to keep doing what we do.

An Hachette UK Company
www.hachette.co.uk

First published in Great Britain in 2019 by
Kyle Books, an imprint of Kyle Cathie Ltd
Carmelite House
50 Victoria Embankment
London EC4Y 0DZ
www.kylebooks.co.uk

ISBN: 978 0 85783 7660

Distributed in the US by Hachette Book Group, 1290 Avenue of the Americas,
4th and 5th Floors, New York, NY 10104

Distributed in Canada by Canadian Manda Group, 664 Annette St., Toronto, Ontario,
Canada M6S 2C8

Publisher: Joanna Copestick
Editor: Tara O'Sullivan
Editorial Assistant: Isabel Gonzalez-Prendergast
Design: Laura Woussen
Photography: Steven Joyce*
Food styling: Rachel de Thample
Props styling: Cynthia Blackett
Production: Nic Jones & Gemma John
*except pages 12–13 (Toby Allen); page 16 (Jutta Klee); page 29 (Glenburn Estate); page 30 (Fiona Kewley);
pages 36–37 (Glenburn Estate); and page 69 (Isabelle Wilkinson)

A Cataloguing in Publication record for this title is available from the British Library

Printed and bound in China

10 9 8 7 6 5 4 3 2 1

Contents

INTRODUCTION

A Good & Proper Story

Good & Proper was established as a business in 2012, but the story began many years earlier. As a non-coffee drinker I was increasingly frustrated by the contrast between the quality and care given to what coffee aficionados were drinking and the disappointing cup I was almost always faced with when ordering tea. I was no tea expert at the time, but I was always surprised to find that taste and consistency were lacking, and presentation was almost universally poor. Having talked for years to no effect about the need to change the way people thought about, made and drank tea, I finally decided to do something about it myself.

Having made the decision in principle, the next step was to take the leap. Armed with little more than instinct and good intentions, I sat at the kitchen table with a basic "to do" list and, before I realized it, I was off. Responses from suppliers started to come in, neat little packages from Japan, China, India, Rwanda and everywhere in between began to arrive by post and, much to the dismay of my flatmates at the time, a lengthy tea-tasting process got underway. Before long, my idea – to create a destination for tea-drinkers – began to take tangible shape and momentum started to build. I knew I wouldn't be able to open a tea bar from the outset so, having seen a growing streetfood movement in London, I decided to find and convert a 1974 Citroën-H van into a mobile tea bar. Although this represented a lower cost of entry than a permanent retail site, it still meant raising funds – funds that I didn't have. In a somewhat serendipitous moment, I saw on Twitter that Kickstarter, the US-based crowdfunding platform, was to launch in the UK. Despite confused reactions I had from friends

and family when trying to explain the concept of rewards-based crowdfunding, I decided I had nothing to lose, and hastily pulled together a project to go live the day Kickstarter launched. We were, it turned out, the very first project to go live on the UK site and, amazingly, we were soon also among the first to be funded. I couldn't have imagined a more extraordinary response – for the next few days my phone buzzed non-stop with emails alerting me to new backers supporting my project. People from all over the world were not only pledging £10 or more to help make it happen, but many were also offering help with fitting out the van, sharing contacts and suggesting places to trade once we were up and running. It seemed I wasn't the only person to be frustrated by a lack of love given to tea, so my backers soon became all-important first ambassadors for what I had set out to do. After a nail-biting five days, I had 372 backers pledging to bring my proposal to life. The van was bought, transformed and equipped – and given the name Watson by a vote among the backers, to fit its Holmesian owner. (The names of each of our backers are still proudly displayed on the back window.)

The first cup of Good & Proper tea was brewed at a market in Shoreditch on a freezing cold day in December 2012. From our first van pitch outside London's King's Cross Station, as part of streetfood community KERB, our itinerant journey took us to festivals and events throughout the country, to pop-ups in London's tokyobike store and Old Street Underground station. In 2015, after turning to the crowd once more, this time with Crowdcube, we opened our first fixed premises – a year-long, tiny but perfectly formed kiosk in Shoreditch. Now, in 2019, thanks to the invaluable help of our customers, friends, partners and suppliers, we have grown to a flagship tea bar in the heart of the capital, an online store and a fast-growing wholesale business – while Watson the van lives on, too.

We have one focus at Good & Proper, which is, of course, the tea. The teas we source are single-origin, meaning that each comes from one geographical region, estate or garden. In their unblended and unflavoured form, the flavour profile of each of those teas is therefore a direct reflection of the soil, the climate, the altitude and aspect of that region – the *terroir*, as it is known in wine – as well as the particular skill that goes into producing it.

We are not the producers of these teas – each is the tireless work of teams in growing regions around the world, who work with nature to bring out the best possible flavour in their crops each year. They craft the teas, while our role is simply to find them – to explore the possibilities and then make choices on our customers' behalf. We hope to bring them some of the best, always ensuring that the integrity and flavour of the leaves are maintained all the way to the cup.

Over the years, we have curated a collection of black, oolong, green and white teas, as well as a range of herbals, each of which brings something different to the table. We look for whole leaf, "orthodox" teas (see page 31) that are representative of their type, their region and their style and then try to find the best possible example for our customers. We are lucky enough to receive regular samples from producers the world over, the leaf and liquor of which are reviewed and tasted at our warehouse in southeast London, each being assessed for quality and flavour. Sometimes, we're simply tasting a new harvest, other times, we're trying something new. And we never stop tasting, so our collection will keep growing...

What Good & Proper Stands For

In setting up Good & Proper Tea, I wanted to show everyone how good tea can be, when things are done right, or "properly". But many years on, this ethos has come to encompass much more than just the tea. It means taking time to get things right, not only in sourcing and brewing the teas, but when serving a customer, dealing with a supplier or simply packing a box for an online order. More often than not that means it takes a bit longer, but it also means nothing is left to chance. And we hope it will lend an honesty and authenticity to the way we do business. It is this approach, I believe, that has earned us the trust of our customers over the years, and it will be even more important as we grow the business that this "good and proper" way of doing things remains at its heart.

Our team see themselves less as tea experts and more as enthusiasts who are always learning. Within the wider tea industry we therefore see our strength as bridging a gap between a nation of tea-drinkers constantly short-changed by what they are being offered, and an exotic world of rituals and traditions not easily open to most people. We will always be fascinated by these age-old traditions, and want to respect and help preserve the cultural richness they embody. But we also know that such things can seem intimidating and even off-putting

for would-be tea enthusiasts. Our aspiration, therefore, is to make all that tea has to offer accessible to everyone, by communicating our passion and enthusiasm for what we have learned, and are still learning.

Over the last seven years, I have been fortunate enough to have had the unsparing support and guiding hands of friends and partners in the industry with far greater expertise than I could ever claim, and each of them has played a role in my own discovery of this extraordinary product. In writing this book, therefore, I hope to share with others the knowledge I have had the privilege of collecting during that time.

I hope you enjoy it and find the subject as exciting and intriguing as my team and I always do.

Our aspiration is to make all that tea has to offer accessible to everyone, by communicating our passion and enthusiasm for what we have learned, and are still learning.

Why Now is the Time for Tea

Here in Britain, we proudly call ourselves a nation of tea-drinkers. We consume vast quantities – around 165 million cups a day – making it the country's favourite hot beverage by some way. Yet tea in the UK is still little understood, and the quality of the tea consumed in the West is, for the most part, very poor. This is now, at last, starting to change, thanks to better appreciation of its merits, trends elsewhere in the food and drink industry, and a new focus on well being.

In many ways we have a lot for which to thank our hot drink rival, coffee. The café culture that Starbucks and others brought into the mainstream back in the eighties has grown and evolved. The arrival of the "third wave" coffee movement has seen fast and frothy cappuccinos and a celebration of the café space pushed aside by so-called "speciality" coffee shops, elevating the coffee bean from commodity to artisanal foodstuff. With it comes a new focus on flavour, provenance and method of brewing. Patrons of these new coffee institutions are looking for more than just their morning caffeine hit – they want a taste of something different and delicious.

The same trend is evident in beer and spirits, with consumers becoming less interested in drinking large volumes of poor-quality drinks, instead looking to "craft" producers offering originality, variety and a new flavour experience. This shift from volume and price to quality and complexity has made connoisseurs of us all and tea is no exception.

The relentless quest for taste has now hit the tea industry, too. Reliance on a standard black tea is no longer enough, with the big players already seeing sales of their basic tea bags stagnate or fall.

Growth is coming instead from an interest in both trading up to higher-quality teas as well as a greater diversity of tea types, with herbal, fruit and green teas leading the charge. This presents an exciting opportunity for new ideas to shape more sophisticated tastes and further stimulate the market, as has happened in recent years with coffee. Boutique tea brands are moving rapidly into this space, and bigger tea brands are also reacting, pushing more premium offers and extending their ranges.

All of this means we are at last starting to reverse long-engrained value perceptions surrounding tea. Customers are now willing to pay more for a better cup and a higher-quality experience. The tea market is not therefore declining, as some have

Growth is coming from an interest in both trading up to higher-quality teas as well as a greater diversity of tea types, with herbal, fruit and green teas leading the charge.

mistakenly reported, but rather evolving fast, and growing in different and fascinating directions.

Meanwhile an important role is also being played by the so-called wellness industry, with new concepts of functional health and clean eating reinforcing moves towards tea. The health benefits of tea have been celebrated for centuries in different societies, but its properties are being appreciated by a new generation of drinkers in the West. The benefits are now acknowledged for both physical and mental health, with today's emphasis on mindfulness an important backdrop to the psychological benefits of tea.

Our own messaging at Good & Proper has been focused more on the simple enjoyment of a good cup of tea – the flavour of the leaves and the drinking experience – than on its appeal as a product doing good to our bodies at the same time. Nevertheless, you would be hard pushed to find an everyday experience offering more benefits for your health. These range from reducing cholesterol and repairing ageing skin cells to aiding digestion and even fighting disease. Green tea in particular saw a rapid growth in sales, thanks to extensive media coverage of its undoubted health properties in recent years.

Tea is also, of course, a simple product of nature. While many products desperately struggle for acceptance through "clean labels", the new holy grail for food and drink startups, tea has nothing to hide. Whatever the level of quality, whether tea bags on the supermarket shelf or loose leaves in a high-end tea retailer, tea is and always has been natural and unadulterated. This super-clean label reinforces its new relevance for younger, "millennial" tea drinkers.

The concept of mindfulness – the practice of tuning into the present moment, of taking a moment to stop and slow down – is also ideally suited to the drinking of tea. Unlike the fast-paced, functional appeal of espresso-based coffee, the ritual of loose leaf tea and the natural time frame it carves out are inherently slow. Both maker and drinker are obliged to take their time, and the experience is correspondingly deeper and more satisfying. Indeed philosophical thought, accompanied by homage to the art of brewing, lies at the core of tea's long cultural history in many countries.

The benefits are seen in both physical and mental health, with today's emphasis on mindfulness an important backdrop to the psychological benefits of tea.

At Good & Proper we have hosted many a morning meditation session at the Tea Bar. The process of watching leaves unfurl as they slowly infuse lends itself perfectly to a moment of reflection. In an increasingly frantic, always connected world, tea has much to offer those looking for such small moments of respite. Indeed, many of those who practise meditation often end their sessions with the ritual of drinking tea. This ability to temper the pace of modern life is yet another reason why new enthusiasts are flocking to this amazing drink.

Those fortunate enough to have travelled in tea-producing regions, and to have seen first hand the people and places behind the leaf, rarely return without a new perspective on tea and a commitment to different ways of drinking. Now this experience is available to all. The limitless variety of teas on offer, and the way in which tea plays so readily into the growing interest in provenance, quality and flavour across the food and drink industry, are attracting new enthusiasts every day. There has never been a more exciting time for tea – and we are only at the start of this journey.

A MINDFUL MOMENT

Start by choosing your tea, whether a black tea to start the day, an oolong to reinvigorate you after lunch or a herbal tea to unwind before bed. Carefully measure your tea into your pot. Be aware of what you are doing, listening to the sound that the kettle makes as the water starts to heat up, eventually bubbling as it approaches boiling point. As you pour the water over the leaves, watch them dance around, slowly unfurling as they release their flavour. Over the course of the infusion, observe how the leaves stain the water with wisps of colour. Once infused, strain the leaves and pour the infusion into your favourite cup, wrapping your hands around it to feel its warmth. Sip slowly, breathe in the aroma and enjoy the complexity of flavour as it hits your taste buds.

RTEA.COM

Tea:
An Overview

Camellia Sinensis:
The One and Only Tea Plant

Despite the millions of cups of tea consumed every day in the UK, it is fair to say that few people know much about what tea is or where it is grown. As we start to take greater interest in where all our food comes from, and to pay more attention to ingredient lists, consumers are only now realizing that tea originates from the leaves and buds of a plant. The proliferation of opaque paper bags containing fine tea "dust" is no doubt partly to blame for this lack of connection, just as instant coffee granules bear little resemblance to coffee beans. The reality is that, behind the cup of tea we prepare every morning, there is a fascinating story, involving people, history and traditions from many parts of the world.

The reality is that, behind the cup of tea we prepare every morning, there is a fascinating story, involving people, history and traditions from all over the world.

Perhaps one of the most surprising things about tea is that all teas come from a single plant. This does not include herbal "teas", *tisanes*, or other recent infusions that have adopted the tea tag – these are made from other plants, herbs or roots. However, all black, oolong, yellow, green and white teas are produced by leaves and buds carefully plucked from the bushes of the *Camellia sinensis*. This evergreen shrub grows best in warm, humid climates with moderate rainfall, but it is impressively adaptable, growing in tropical and subtropical parts of the world, from sea level up to altitudes of 2,100 metres (nearly 7,000 feet). It thrives in regions with marked seasons, meaning there are distinct dry and wet periods.

Although *Camellia sinensis* is one plant, in tea we talk about two predominant and distinct varieties: *assamica* and *sinensis*. The former, native to Assam, the state in northeast India from which it takes its name, thrives in the region's high humidity and high rainfall and is also the preferred crop in the tea-growing areas of Africa and Sri Lanka. At their best, the large, thick leaves of *assamica* can be plucked year-round, offering a generous and robust yield, best suited to teas undergoing a heavy production process, such as black teas and some oolongs.

The *sinensis* variety, by contrast, often referred to as the "China" cultivar, thrives at higher altitudes in cooler temperatures. It is often found growing on steep slopes, such as those in Darjeeling or mountainous areas of China, where the growing seasons tend to be shorter and more marked. At these altitudes, yields are lower and the leaves smaller and more delicate, with the bushes only being plucked a handful of times a year. What they lack in consistency and volume, however, they more than make up for in unique flavour profiles.

PLUCKING

The leaves of the tea bushes are collected through regular plucking – that is the removal of the top young leaves and buds – which is as much about maintaining the bushes as it is about harvesting leaves for production. First, it prevents the bushes from flowering. Although beautiful, allowing the white and yellow flowers to bloom diverts some of the plant's energy away from producing the sap that gives tea its sweetness. Secondly, tea plants left unattended can grow to heights of up to 30 metres (almost 100 feet). Most cultivated tea bushes are maintained at a consistent height of around 2 metres (6 feet) for ease of harvesting and to ensure even exposure to sunlight. This level surface is known as the "plucking table". The way the tea is harvested plays an important role in the quality of the final product. Only by carefully selecting the best leaves – often the top one or two young leaves and a bud – and leaving the tougher, more mature leaves and stems, can a high-quality tea be produced. This is called the "plucking standard".

Plucking itself is a skill requiring dexterity, speed and a good eye. Many believe it can only be done by hand for the best results. However, a single tea-picker's daily harvest of up to 20kg (44lb) of green leaves yields just 5kg (11lb) of finished tea, making this labour-intensive task performed by highly skilled pickers the most significant cost in the production of tea. It is no surprise, therefore, that the industry is seeking to move to mechanized harvesting solutions. The timing of the harvest is also key. It varies from region to region, and from season to season,

Only by carefully selecting the best leaves – often the top one or two young leaves and a bud – and leaving the tougher, more mature leaves and stems, can a high-quality tea be produced.

according to variations in sunlight and rainfall. Getting the timing right is critical as the window of opportunity during which the buds first appear and open, before they grow into large, tougher leaves, is short. If the opportunity is missed, even just by a few days, the quality may well be compromised. The period during the year at which the tea is picked will also be reflected in its characteristics. For example, the first harvests of the year, known as the first flush in India, *shincha* (meaning new tea) in Japan and *pre-Qing Ming* in China, are highly prized. After a long period of dormancy over the winter months, during which time nutrients have been able to build up in the plant, the young sappy leaves produce particularly unique flavour

profiles. The thrill of tasting the first of the year's tea is eagerly anticipated, with enthusiasts ever hopeful of a delicious year ahead.

Picking the right leaves, however, is of course only the beginning. As with grapes and wine, the art of the tea producer lies in making sure that every step of the production process is done with the same precision in order that the flavour in the leaves is both maintained and ultimately enhanced. This is a genuine skill, even an art, that needs to be achieved at a cost that will ensure the final tea, now a highly sought-after product, remains competitive in the global market.

As with grapes and wine, the art of the tea producer lies in making sure that every step of the production process is done with the same precision, in order that the flavour of the leaves is both maintained and ultimately enhanced.

ORTHODOX VS. CTC

There are two distinct styles of tea manufacture. So-called 'Orthodox' teas undergo a process akin to the traditional method of hand rolling. A rolling machine gently presses the leaves, bruising and twisting them in order to break down the cell structures in the leaf. The leaves are not overworked, but the rolling action encourages the natural enzymes in the leaf to react with oxygen and so begins the process of oxidation. Large-scale operations, by contrast, use what is known as CTC (or Cut, Tear, Curl), a process designed in the 1950s to meet the market demand for rapidly proliferating tea bags. The leaves are fed through large rollers with sharp teeth that crush and shred them. The process is repeated until the leaf is broken into uniform pieces. Tea destined for commercial tea bags is almost always treated in this way.

Growing Regions: The Impact of Provenance on Flavour

When we talk about wine, we are well versed in the nuances that the grape-producing region brings to the glass. Winemakers and buyers alike speak knowledgeably and enthusiastically about *terroir* – the subtle variations in geology, slope, altitude and climate – and its impact on the product. Why should it be any different when the product is tea rather than grapes?

Part of the reason we're unaware of the link between provenance and tea is because the origins have been long hidden behind blends. The label of an English Breakfast tea, for example, often promises body and strength, but offers little or no information about what the component ingredients are and what they do to give the blend its characteristics. And, understandably, the bigger tea companies have focused on providing their customers with a consistent flavour, year on year, above all else. They have therefore tweaked the blend "recipe" or balance of origins in order to smooth over the variations that different seasons or harvests inevitably bring. In fairness, it is also only recently that customers have shown real interest in the subject, following a wider trend towards knowing more about the provenance of food and drink.

Along with unique local traditions and production techniques, the geographical nuances of the region of origin are central to determining the flavour, aroma and key characteristics of any given tea. This is what makes single-origin teas, just like single-origin coffee or chocolate, so exciting – each cup is a direct expression of the area in which those particular leaves were grown.

This is what makes single-origin teas so exciting – each cup is a direct expression of the area in which those particular leaves were grown.

In order to navigate your way through a tea menu and know where your own preferences lie, it is essential to understand the key attributes of some of the world's most important tea-growing regions.

CHINA

By almost all measures China is the most important tea-growing region in the world. Covering the full spectrum of tea types, it is comfortably the largest producer in the world by annual volume; in fact only a few provinces – generally in the cold arid north bordering Mongolia – do not grow tea. The history of tea consumption spans many centuries and China is widely believed to be the birthplace of tea. The *terroir* breadth of this vast country, from steep mountain slopes to ancient forests and fertile plains, means the range and variety of teas grown in China are too numerous to be covered in any depth here. Most famous, perhaps, for its myriad greens and oolongs, China also has a rich pedigree of black teas. Keemun and Yunnan are two of the best-known examples.

The best pickings tend to come from four regions: Jiangbei, Jiangnan, the southwest and the south.

Jiangnan

Jiangnan, the region immediately south of the Yangtze River, from Shanghai south to the border with Vietnam, is responsible for the production of around two-thirds of all Chinese tea. It is a region where average temperatures are high, and most of the tea grown is produced in the mountains at altitudes that experience four very distinct seasons: plenty of rain in spring and summer, followed by dry autumns and winters. This seasonality lends itself to a wonderfully diverse output in terms of the teas produced here. Of particular note are Dragon Well (or *Long Jing*), a handmade-wok-fired green tea which often tops the list as one of China's so called "ten famous teas"; Keemun (or *Qimen*), perhaps China's most celebrated black tea; and Phoenix Honey Orchid (or *Mi Lan Dan Cong*), an exquisitely fragrant dark oolong picked from wild trees on Phoenix Mountain in Guangdong Province.

Jiangbei

In contrast to Jiangnan, Jiangbei, north of the Yangtze, has much lower year-round temperatures and less rainfall. It is the most northerly of the tea-producing regions of China and its climate is well-suited to slower-growing green teas. *Mao Jian* green tea, or what we call Jade Tips, is one of the best-known teas from the region, its dark green leaves producing a clean, floral cup.

Southwest

Despite variations in altitude, the southwest of China has a relatively stable climate and includes what is believed to be the birthplace of tea, Yunnan province. The speciality here is Puer tea, a style of fermented and compressed tea unique to this area, the best examples of which are found in the mountainous area of southern Yunnan, bordering both Myanmar and Laos. Puer derives its flavour as much from the ageing process as it does from the *terroir*, with ancient tea trees growing here nourished by rich, organic soil. Teas from this area, when crafted with skill, can be wonderfully rich and earthy. Their particular truffle-like aroma is beloved by devotees of these unusual fermented teas. Another of China's renowned black teas, *Dianhong*, or simply "Yunnan", is also produced here, a full-bodied black tea with a nutty, even smoky finish.

South Coast

Finally, the area on the southeast coast of mainland China boasts the country's finest tea-growing conditions, thanks to a long growing season, cool temperatures and plenty of rain. Black, oolong and white teas are all produced here, with the local red clay giving oolongs, such as *Tie Guan Yin* (Iron Goddess of Mercy) and Wuyi Rock, their body and rich flavour. Silver Needle, produced in the counties around Fuding, is another tea of particular note from this area. Produced from locally cultivated *Da Bai* (or Big White) bushes, these silver, downy buds produce a light, delicately sweet tea that has become one of the most highly prized teas in the world.

 INDIA

Many tea lovers consider India to be the high church of black tea. Indian tea was first commercialized by the British in the early nineteenth century as an alternative to China to meet Britain's insatiable demand for tea, which was driving up prices. India is now one of the largest tea producers in the world.

India boasts as many tea estates producing high-quality, "orthodox" tea as there are farms producing cut-tear-curl or CTC (see page 31) for mass-market tea bags. Indeed most estates produce both, with the latter sold daily via auction and still forming the bread and butter of their businesses. India has three main growing areas: Darjeeling, Assam and Nilgiri, each with its own distinct *terroir*.

Darjeeling

Darjeeling, a remote part of West Bengal at the foot of the Himalayas, is one of the highest tea-growing regions in the world and perhaps one of the most unique. The area is characterized by vertiginous slopes, making picking an unenviable task. As a result, mass production is impossible here, with only the most dedicated and passionate farmers harvesting and producing the leaves that are revered the world over. The altitude and the cold winds that blow south from the mountains keep the area cool and the tea growth slow, which in turn gives Darjeeling its complexity and unique "muscatel" or wine-like character.

Assam

Assam, by contrast, is the single largest tea-producing region in the world. Nestled in the far northeastern corner of India, bordering Bhutan to the north, Assam has high humidity and exceptionally high rainfall. Unlike the steeply

sloped terraces of Darjeeling, estates here sit on flat plains around the winding Brahmaputra river. When it floods, this vast stretch of water gives the local soil a richness that is mirrored in the coppery liquors of the tea it nourishes. Much of Assam production is given over to CTC (see page 31). Its part in an English Breakfast blend is what gives the cup its all-important colour and body. For more complex, honey-sweet Assams, whole leaf "tippy" orthodox teas should be sought out, an abundance of tips or young leaf buds providing extra sweetness.

Nilgiri

Less well known than either Assam or Darjeeling, Nilgiri, the tea-growing region on the southwestern tip of India, offers something different again and represents around a quarter of India's production. The high elevation, high rainfall and high humidity of this lush jungle region give tea from the Nilgiri Mountains a bright, aromatic character more akin to a Ceylon tea than other Indian teas. While the majority is still produced using CTC production methods, the region also produces quality orthodox teas. Of particular interest is the so-called "frost tea", tea from leaves picked in the winter months, immediately following a frost. The trauma of the cold temperature causes the plant to produce compounds as a defence mechanism, which encourage more sweetness in the leaf.

SRI LANKA

The relatively small island off the southeastern tip of India is the fourth-largest tea producer in the world – a ranking that is all the more impressive when we consider that until the late nineteenth century Sri Lanka had little or no tea farming at all. The land was instead dedicated to the production of coffee until its plantations were wiped out by disease in 1870. An enterprising Briton, James Thomas, who was living in Sri Lanka at the time of the coffee disaster, saw the fledgling tea industry in neighbouring India and decided to try his own luck at growing tea. The first of his imported seedlings was planted in 1867, and his experiment paid off handsomely; the tea plants flourished and what is now trademarked as Ceylon tea was born.

Sri Lanka, or Ceylon as it continues to be known in the tea world, produces predominantly black tea and its humid, tropical climate means tea can be harvested almost all year round. Perhaps the most interesting aspect of Sri Lanka as a growing region is the island's microclimates, most notably its elevations, with tea growing from sea level up to altitudes of over 2,000 metres (6,800 feet). Low-grown teas are characterized by thick, wiry leaves, producing a full-bodied, almost smoky cup with a strong, dark liquor. By contrast, teas grown high in the mountains, such as those from the island's highest producing region, Nuwara Eliya, are generally considered to be the crown jewel in Sri Lanka's production, producing more delicate, crisp, aromatic cups. The British, longstanding enthusiastic consumers of Ceylon black teas, have found a happy medium for their palate in the shape of the medium-bodied brisk and bright teas produced in the mid–high regions of Uva and Dimbula in particular.

AFRICA

Much of Africa has ideal tea-growing conditions. While the best results come from tea picked during the drier months, its tropical and sub-tropical climate means the continent benefits from a year-round harvest. Historically, however, Africa has had a poor reputation when it comes to tea, due to a predominance of CTC production for large commodity tea brokers and a focus on high-volume tea destined for cheap and cheerful tea bags. This has meant that African teas, though widely consumed within breakfast blends (the iconic UK brand Yorkshire Tea, for example, owes its much-loved strength to a high proportion of Kenyan tea), are only now being actively sought out. Tea drinkers might have previously considered Rooibos (a herbal infusion unique to Southern Africa) to be the region's greatest tea export, but that mistake is now being corrected.

East African countries – Kenya, Rwanda and Malawi in particular – are tea producers that cannot be ignored, and are most celebrated for robust black teas that are well suited to milk. If that is your preference, you will be hard pushed to find a livelier breakfast cup than those from the best producers in Kenya, particularly from those with plantations on the southern slopes of Mount

Kenya. Unlike India, where estates typically own and operate their own processing facilities, in Kenya much of the crop is grown and harvested by smallholders, then sold as green leaf to independent factories for production. The volcanic soils in Rwanda, where tea is now the largest export and a significant part of the economy, are particularly favourable to tea production and the country's best teas have a golden, honey-like liquor. Finally, in landlocked Malawi, Africa's oldest tea-producing region, plentiful rain in the peak growing season has resulted in a thriving trade in black tea. In some years, erratic climate conditions, such as droughts caused by El Niño, can result in poor yields, but when the conditions are right, so is the tea. Its bright red liquors and robust flavour make for an exciting cup.

JAPAN

In Japan, tea is elevated to an almost spiritual level at every stage of its evolution from bush to cup. The traditional Japanese tea ceremony, known as *chado* or "the way of tea", turns the simple gesture of exchanging refreshment between guest and host into an artform, with mindfulness and zen philosophy at the core of both its preparation and consumption.

Green teas, which make up the vast majority of the country's production, are highly regarded the world over, from grassy Senchas and Gyokuros to nutty Hojichas and Genmaichas. The country also produces the unique stoneground green tea, Matcha, Japan's fastest-growing tea export. Despite high regard in the global tea world, 90 per cent of Japanese tea production is for domestic consumption.

The climate is humid, ranging from cool temperatures in the north to subtropical conditions in the south, with volcanic soils and exposure to sea air both contributing to the unique umami flavours and seaweed character that green tea enthusiasts seek from the best Japanese teas. Tea is widely grown across the country, but the majority is produced in the Shizuoka, Mie and Kagoshima prefectures. Some of Japan's most exquisite teas, however, come from farms in the Kyoto Prefecture. The unique *terroir* notwithstanding, a steaming process during production also typifies Japanese green teas. This process retains much of the vibrant green colour and bright, grassy flavours of the leaf, with the sweet-savoury balance of a good Sencha being the best representation.

Tea and its Types – What They Are and How They're Made

The source of all teas, whether black, oolong, green, yellow or white, is the leaves and buds plucked from a single plant, Camellia sinensis. What happens to the plucked leaves during the subsequent processing stage determines which type of tea it becomes. These types share common characteristics, so it is important to understand the nuances of each as well as looking at the importance of geographical origin in determining a tea's unique flavour and aroma.

BLACK

The distinguishing feature of black tea production is the full oxidation of the freshly plucked tea leaf. This results in dark, robust flavours, ranging from India's rich, malty Assams through China's Keemuns, with their bittersweet notes of dark chocolate, to East Africa's single-origin black teas with lively hints of fruit and caramel.

Turning freshly plucked green tea leaves into the familiar dark leaves of a black tea involves a number of steps: withering, rolling, oxidizing, drying, then finally sorting and packing. It is the rolling and oxidation of the leaves in particular that define a black tea (confusingly known in China as a "red tea", owing to the dark red liquors they produce).

Once picked, the green leaves are transported to the factory where they undergo a process of withering. The leaves are laid out, usually in large troughs, and warm air is circulated around them, encouraging the moisture both on the surface and inside the leaf to evaporate. In

doing so the leaves become soft and malleable, which is important for the process that follows.

The next stage, rolling the leaves, can be done in one of two ways, depending on the style of manufacture. Orthodox teas undergo a process akin to the traditional method of hand rolling. A rolling machine gently presses the leaves, bruising and twisting them in order to break down the cell structures in the leaf. The leaves are not overworked, ensuring they remain intact, but the rolling action encourages the natural enzymes in the leaf to react with oxygen in the air and so begins the process of oxidation.

Large-scale operations, by contrast, use what is known as CTC (or Cut, Tear, Curl), a process designed in the 1950s to meet the market demand for rapidly proliferating tea bags. Rather than the leaves being rolled, they are fed through large rollers with sharp teeth that simultaneously crush and shred the leaves. The process is repeated multiple times until the leaf is broken into uniform pieces. Tea destined for commercial tea bags is almost always treated in this way, because the smaller leaf size and the speed and efficiency of the process were important factors in developing what soon became a commodity product. Though there are losses in complexity and flavour using this

process compared to tea manufactured using traditional methods, there is a time and a place for some of the best CTC teas, which have a strength and full body that are hard to beat with a splash of milk.

After rolling or CTC, the next stage of oxidation is perhaps the most defining in black tea production. It is simply the process of enzymes in the leaf encountering oxygen, in the same way that a peeled apple turns brown when exposed to air. For black tea the leaves are encouraged to fully oxidize, and so develop the typically rich, robust characteristics of this type of tea.

Once the oxidation is deemed complete, the process is then stopped or "fixed" by drying the tea. Generally for black teas, leaves are fed into a furnace or dryer, where the high temperature in the heated chamber halts the oxidation process, ensuring the key characteristics of that particular tea are locked in place.

Finally, the dried tea needs to be sorted and packed. Until this point, the tea has been treated as a single batch of leaf shapes and sizes, particularly during orthodox production. However, the stalks and detritus that inevitably were mixed in with the leaves must now be removed, before the remaining leaves are sized and graded for packing.

OOLONG

Oolong teas are semi-oxidized, meaning that the process of oxidation is halted at a controlled point. This varying level of oxidation and the craft involved in oolong production is what makes this tea type so exciting, with a huge spectrum of flavours. Expect everything from delicate floral and tropical fruit notes from lighter, "green" oolongs to black cherry and cacao from their darker, more heavily oxidized, counterparts.

Oolong (or *Wu Long*), meaning "black dragon", is, in terms of oxidation, a simple halfway house between black and green tea. However, the skill and time required to craft the best oolongs make this tea type unique.

After picking, the leaves are first withered on mats in the sun. This process should take up to an hour but, unlike indoor withering, the maker of oolong tea is at the mercy of the elements. In particularly hot climes, for instance, shade is needed to regulate the temperature and speed of drying. After this initial solar withering, the leaves are brought inside for a more traditional withering for up to 8 hours. This dual withering process encourages the development of floral characteristics on the finished leaves.

The next stage of production, equivalent to rolling for black teas, is unique to oolong. The leaves are poured into a large basket or bamboo drum and shaken vigorously to break down the cell structures in the leaf and so kickstart oxidation. The leaves are then left to oxidize, the duration of which determines the flavour of the finished product, with levels of oxidation anywhere from around 10 per cent for a so-called "green" oolong and up to 80 per cent for a classic Formosa or "dark" oolong. The partially oxidized leaves are then "panned" using dry heat to halt the process once more.

The final stages are dependent on the style of oolong being produced and the desired outcome of the maker. One key characteristic of an oolong is the shape, so the leaves might be rolled and twisted before being dried completely, or for "balled" oolongs they might be rolled, partially dried, then wrapped in large cloth bags. For the latter, the rolling, drying, wrapping and unwrapping is repeated multiple times until tight nuggets are formed. The leaves may also be roasted or baked, encouraging the development of body, aroma and characteristic toasted flavours. The lengthy processes involved require considerable skill on the part of the makers, and the success of the best oolongs therefore rests squarely on their mastery of technique and timing.

GREEN

Green tea production avoids oxidation altogether. This is why green tea has a vibrant green colour and fresh, vegetal character. Green teas are surprisingly diverse, ranging from the sweet, floral character of a Chinese green, to an intense, sweet–savoury Japanese Sencha, their flavour a reflection of both where the leaves were grown and how they were manufactured.

Compared with black tea, green tea production is relatively simple. The focus is to prevent oxidation entirely and instead deactivate the enzymes in the leaf as early as possible.

After the leaves are plucked, they undergo a light withering. This can be done in the open air, using the sun to absorb moisture from the leaf, leading to more floral characteristics. However, as this process starts to activate the enzymes, speed is of the essence. Immediately afterwards, heat is used to "fix" the tea, stopping the oxidation in its tracks – a process known as "kill-green". This is usually done by either pan-firing, which is the predominant method used in China, or steaming, the preferred method in Japan. The chosen method of fixing the tea has a dramatic impact on its flavour.

For pan-fired green teas, the leaves, once withered, are introduced to a large pan that sits over a high heat. As the leaves are tossed and rubbed into the hot surface, the enzymes are deactivated and oxidation ceases. For larger-scale production, this process is replicated in a mechanized drum. Care has to be taken to heat the leaf enough to stop the oxidation, but not so much that the tea "catches", resulting in burnt, toasty notes that can be tasted in the finished product.

For steamed green teas, steam replaces the heat of the pan as the method of kill-green. The main variable here is the time the leaves are left to steam. Short exposures of up to 30 seconds lead to intense, lightly astringent teas, whereas a longer steaming of up to 2 minutes encourages more sweetness and grassiness from the tea, but less intensity. As always, there is a balance to be found, and that is the skill of the maker.

As the leaves exit the steaming process soft and wet, subsequent rolling and drying of the leaves is required. These days this, like the steaming itself, is almost always mechanized. The machines shape, dry and roll the leaves while removing almost all the remaining moisture. It is through this process that the long needle-like leaves we recognise as Sencha are created.

WHITE

The least processed of all tea types, white teas are highly prized the world over. Only the youngest, finest leaves and buds are painstakingly plucked, before being gently withered and dried. The result is a pale, champagne-coloured cup with a uniquely fresh, delicate flavour. From the best white teas you will find character ranging from the gentle honeysuckle of Silver Needle, to the more full-bodied White Peony, brimming with melon-like sweetness.

Traditionally, white tea refers to the young leaves and buds plucked from *Da Bai* (Big White) bushes, a cultivar of the tea plant growing in Fujian province, China, characterized by the downy white hairs that cover their surfaces. The best leaves and buds are harvested in spring, before being gently withered. The majority of producers use a combination of indoor and solar withering to control the process and allow just the right amount of initial oxidation of the leaf. Many tea drinkers mistakenly believe that white teas are the least oxidized of all tea types, but in fact, while the maker will neither provoke nor prevent it, natural oxidation does occur during the wither. Unlike the oolongs, the withering process for white tea is long and gentle, and this is where much of the intensity of its characteristic aroma and sweetness develops.

When the leaves are deemed ready, white tea is dried, again very gently, with a focus on keeping whole buds and leaves intact throughout. Once dried, the sorting and packing of white tea is equally as meticulous, with some producers still using manual sorting to ensure only the best leaves and buds are selected for sale. Such a long and careful production process means the best white teas are both highly prized and highly priced, but for their unique sweetness and delicate aroma, the best are very much worth the effort.

PUER

The fermentation and ageing process of Puer tea is what gives it its extraordinary character; potent, smooth, rounded and complex, yet retaining the vibrancy of the young fresh leaf, the best Puer teas are characteristically earthy, deep and full of life.

Puer is unique for many reasons. It is a dark tea that is processed largely as a green tea, it is often sold in compressed cakes as opposed to the dried loose leaves we are used to, and it courts and manipulates yeast, mould and bacteria to develop aromas not found in any other style of tea.

Almost all Puer tea comes from China, the majority coming from Yunnan province, where the leaves of ancient wild tea trees have the potential for rich, woody and earthy characters if handled correctly.

Leaves destined to make Puer are laid out and solar withered. They are then pan-roasted, like many Chinese green teas, to stop the oxidation in its tracks. However, the difference between Puer and green teas is that the producer does not want the enzyme activity stopped entirely. The aim is to stop the oxidation at this point, but to keep alive as much bacteria as possible within the leaf to ensure a vigorous fermentation in the final process for making Puer tea.

Once the tea has been withered and dried it is either made into *Sheng*, or "raw" Puer, or produced via a more modern method into *Shou*, or "cooked" Puer. The former is compressed into cakes which are then stacked and left to ferment and mature in warm, humid conditions – a process that can take years to achieve the best flavours. For the latter, the leaves are piled and covered, then turned and re-covered, hastening the process of fermentation, before being packed into cakes and wrapped to be sold. Both processes are designed to encourage the deep earthy character that is expected from Puer.

The very best "raw" Puer teas can be aged as cakes for 30 or more years, and like fine wine, the intensity and complexity of flavour is matched by a hefty price tag. For most of us, it is more likely that a young or "cooked" Puer will be within our reach. The complexity of flavour might not be as rousing as a rare, aged Puer, but the unique and deep character will be enough to hook you and have you dreaming of those 30-year aged cakes.

HERBAL

Herbal teas or *tisanes* offer a rainbow of colours and a wide spectrum of flavours to match. Expect anything from a fresh, palate-cleansing Peppermint to a zingy Lemongrass, a calming, honey-sweet Chamomile to a sweet–sour Hibiscus.

Herbal teas have never been so popular, with tea drinkers increasingly switching to herbs when looking to reduce their caffeine intake, as well as taking advantage of their many reported health benefits.

Unlike all other tea types, such as black, oolong, green and white, herbal "teas" do not actually come from the tea plant, *Camellia sinensis*. Strictly speaking, herbs shouldn't really be called teas at all, but rather infusions or *tisanes*, as they all come from different plants, each one distinct in flavour and properties. A herbal tea is therefore simply an infusion of a particular herb in hot water.

Herbal teas can be made from fresh or dried flowers, leaves, seeds or even roots. For example, Hibiscus tea is made from whole hibiscus flowers, which are picked and simply dried in the sun. Chamomile is treated in a similar way. Peppermint and Lemon Verbena teas are made with leaves from their respective plants and Lemongrass tea is made with the picked and dried root of the same plant. Aside from South Africa's Rooibos, which undergoes oxidation much like a traditional tea, the process for herbal tea production is usually simple, and its main focus is on drying, and thus preserving, the flower, leaf or root, and the flavour it contains.

Mastering the Brew

Thanks to an explosion of cafés on our high streets, and particularly the growth in the speciality coffee shop sector, we now take it as a given that coffee beans must be treated with respect and that it requires highly skilled baristas and expensive equipment to extract the best flavour from every bean. After all, that's why we've become accustomed to paying for the luxury of someone else making it for us. Well, it may surprise you to know that tea leaves are perhaps even more demanding than coffee beans. While there should be no doubt that poor-quality leaves can never be saved by careful brewing, it is equally true that the most exquisite tea in the world can quickly and easily be ruined by getting it wrong. There are, therefore, a few things worth considering before preparing your next cup in order to get the best from your leaves.

Water Quality

Whether you're a loose leaf aficionado or make your morning cup with tea bags, you'll know that to make a cup of tea you only need two things – the tea itself and hot water. Getting the water right, therefore, can make the difference between a good cup and an unpalatable one – bad water making even the best leaves taste lacklustre.

FRESHLY DRAWN WATER

For the liveliest cup of tea you'll need freshly drawn water. That means don't just flip the switch on your kettle and reheat water that's been sitting there already – fill your kettle afresh. The best flavour is drawn out of the tea leaves using oxygen-rich water. Water that has been sitting a while, or more likely boiled over and over again, will lack oxygen, leaving your cup of tea tasting flat. Not only is this one of the easiest ways to improve your morning brew, it is also a good one to get right for the sake of the environment. Although ditching full kettles of old water is no good thing, according to the Energy Saving Trust, if we all got into the habit of filling the kettle with only as much water as we need (rather than filling it to the top each time) that could save enough electricity in a year to power nearly half of all the street lighting in the UK.

HARD OR SOFT WATER?

Truth be told, tea will always taste at its absolute best when brewed using the same local spring water that is used to nurture the tea plants at origin, but that's no use to us at home! Depending on where you live, you'll likely know whether your area has hard or soft water. For example, unfortunately for Londoners, the water is very hard due to the high levels of naturally occurring calcium carbonate (the chalky substance that causes limescale) and magnesium compounds, making it a less than ideal starting point for tea. This mineral-rich, hard water is alkaline and tends to produce a thick, chalky and sometimes even metallic-tasting cup. It is also slow and inefficient at extracting flavour. Soft water, on the other hand, is acidic. Though that makes it much more efficient in dissolving flavour, it tends to happen too quickly, meaning your brew will often over extract, leaving it tasting bitter and astringent. There is a happy medium to be found – as close to pure spring water as possible in terms of acidity, with a pH of around 7. If your local tap water is excessively hard or soft, therefore, you'll need to filter it. You'll be amazed by how much more vibrant the tea looks, and how much more you'll taste in the cup.

Water Temperature

Now you've got the water quality sussed, it's time to think about the temperature of that water. Different teas brew best at different temperatures and getting it right can be the difference between a deliciously smooth cup and an unpleasantly bitter one. For example, green teas contain high levels of amino acids, responsible for sweetness and fresh, delicate aromas, as well as polyphenols, such as tannins, which deliver more astringent, bitter characteristics. While the latter are dissolved in water just off the boil, amino acids dissolve at around 60°C (140°F), so to bring out the most desirable sweet, fresh flavour notes of a green tea, we need to lower the temperature of the water. Making this simple adjustment often turns a green tea hater into a fanatic, because green teas brewed with boiling water – as they so often are in the UK – can be unpleasantly bitter.

On the other hand, water that is not hot enough can, for other teas, leave your cup lacking. Those same polyphenols are key to delivering flavour in black teas and they are not released unless the water is just off the boil. To get the full flavour that the description of the tea promises, you're therefore best following the instructions carefully in this book. As a general rule of thumb, black teas and herbs like heat, while oolongs, greens and whites need you to bring the temperature down. You can achieve this at home by either switching off the kettle before it reaches a boil, or by flipping the lid of the kettle once boiled and allowing the water a few minutes to cool before pouring it over the leaves. Even better – get yourself a temperature-controlled kettle.

For hundreds of years, the Chinese have simply watched the water as it is heated in order to determine the temperature, observing the way the water, and more specifically the size of the bubbles, changes as the temperature rises. So if you've got a glass kettle or even a pan on the hob, use this simple method for getting the water temperature right for your type of tea:

"Shrimp eyes"
The first small bubbles appear on the base of the pan – 70°C (158°F)

"Crab eyes"
The bubbles have expanded to the size of crabs' eyes, with the first wisps of steam coming off the surface of the water – 80°C (176°F)

"Fish eyes"
The bubbles grow larger still and now start to gently rise to the surface – 85°C (185°F)

"String of pearls"
Streams of bubbles now rise to the surface – 95°C (200°F)

"Raging torrent"
What we call a rolling boiil – 100°C (212°F)

Brewing Kit

On entering the exciting world of flavour that is loose leaf tea, one of the things new converts find most intimidating is what to brew the leaves in. Unlike the convenient tea bag, which is neatly pre-dosed and can be quickly whipped out of the mug when the desired strength is reached, loose leaf tea requires a little more care. Most importantly, the leaves need plenty of room to unfurl in order to release their flavour. They also benefit from sufficient space so that the water can move around them as it infuses. Thankfully, centuries of tea-making have ensured that there is no shortage of options when it comes to brewing kit.

Perhaps the easiest method, requiring little or no kit at all, is brewing "naked". Simply place the leaves inside your pot, top up with hot water and then strain the tea leaves using a mesh strainer as you pour into your cup. For a single serving, this works brilliantly – the leaves have had plenty of space to move around and at the end of the infusion, all of the liquor is separated from the leaf. However, if you're making more than one cup, the remaining water in the pot will continue to extract flavour from the leaf as you enjoy the first, leaving your second cup unpleasantly bitter.

The solution is a generously sized infuser basket, which allows as much room as possible for the leaves when brewing, but allows you to easily pull them out, much like a tea bag, once the tea is ready. You can even put them in again for a second infusion. These baskets can sit neatly inside your favourite mug for a single cup but some glass and ceramic teapots now come with removable infuser baskets built in. While glass infusers look beautiful, they rarely last long with daily use, so stainless steel is best – both for practicality and to avoid any taint to the flavour. The ubiquitous stainless-steel tea "balls" or infuser tongs can work for smaller leaf teas, but be careful not to overload them. Wet leaf expands to up to five times the volume of its dry leaf form and, if packed too tight, the leaves will squeeze out bitter tannins into your tea.

These two options are best suited to Western style brewing methods – that is mostly single infusions with longer brewing times. However, East Asian tea-making tends towards multiple short infusions and a high ratio of leaf to water designed to showcase the different and evolving flavour profiles of any given tea. Here the perfect tool is the traditional Chinese *gaiwan* – a simple ceramic lidded cup, with the lid serving to hold back the leaves when pouring out the tea.

For anyone looking to enhance their brewing experience even further, traditional teapots are hard to resist and make for wonderful brewing companions. A Chinese *Yixing* teapot is a tiny clay pot. In time, its unglazed walls take on the flavours of the tea, making for an even more delicious cup. Similarly, Japanese *kyusu* teapots, the best of which are beautifully crafted by local artisans, are well suited to brewing Japanese green teas with

high quantities of leaves. Most of these pots have holes around the spout on the inside, catching the leaves as you pour.

Whichever pot you choose, a set of pocket scales to measure the right amount of leaves, as well as a timer of some description to time the infusion, are both helpful tools to ensure you're getting the best out of your tea.

Centuries of tea-making have ensured that there is no shortage of options when it comes to brewing kit.

Caffeine

We are often asked by customers how much caffeine there is in tea, but the answer is not straightforward. Several factors interplay to determine the amount of caffeine absorbed by the body when drinking tea, and the additional presence of natural amino acids means that the caffeine released in a cup of tea will affect the body differently from the equivalent amount in a cup of coffee.

WHAT IS CAFFEINE?

Caffeine is a stimulant that activates the heart and nervous system, providing energy, heightened alertness and increased mental and physical endurance levels. It is a naturally occurring substance found in the leaves, seeds and fruits of many plants, but most commonly in coffee, cocoa beans and tea leaves, where it occurs as a natural pesticide, protecting them from insects that attempt to eat the plant.

Once ingested, caffeine is absorbed into the blood and body tissues in around thirty minutes. This then disrupts the function of one of the body's key sleep-inducing molecules, adenosine, which, when uninhibited, causes us to feel sluggish. Caffeine blocks adenosine from functioning, and in doing so acts as a stimulant.

The caffeine content in each cup of tea is dependent on four main factors:

• *Terroir* – that is where the tea was grown, the soil, the climate, the altitude – plays a role in the caffeine content in any given tea. The young bud and first leaf of a plant also tend to have slightly more caffeine than leaves picked from the lower part of the tea bush.

• A higher quantity of tea used per cup results in a higher caffeine content. Black teas, for example, tend to require the most dry leaf per cup – roughly 3g for a 200ml (7fl oz) pot – compared to 2.5g for some oolongs.

• The brewing temperature also affects the amount of caffeine that is released into the cup. A lower water temperature will result in less caffeine than in a cup of tea that has been brewed in water just off the boil.

• How long the leaves are infused for is also an important factor. The longer a tea is steeped for, the more caffeine is released into the liquor, so a tea that is left to brew for only 2 minutes will result in a less-caffeinated cup. There is, therefore, some truth in us crying out for a really strong cuppa when we need that extra push to get us going in the morning.

HOW DOES CAFFEINE IN TEA COMPARE WITH THAT IN COFFEE?

Caffeinated tea affects the body differently from coffee. The former is like having a bowl of porridge for breakfast, the latter a bar of chocolate. Both will give you energy, but while coffee will release it quickly, often swiftly followed by a crash, the tea's "energy" will be released slowly, over a much longer period of time. This is largely because, as well as caffeine, tea also contains L-theanine, a natural amino acid that not only has calming properties of its own, but also slows down the release of caffeine into the bloodstream. The presence of both therefore results in a more balanced energy experience.

Another contributing factor is the amount of raw ingredient that goes into making a cup of tea compared with coffee. Although on a dry weight basis tea often contains more caffeine than coffee, far less dry leaf is needed to make a cup of tea than coffee beans are required to make a coffee. To brew an Earl Grey, for example, we might use 3.5g of loose leaf for a 200ml (7fl oz) mug, while a coffee of the same size would require more like 16g of ground coffee.

Brewing Time

Brewing time – that is, the period in which the leaves and water are in contact – plays an important role in extracting flavour, and getting it right is another essential feature of a delicious cup of tea. Many tea bags contain fine leaf grades or "dust", designed for strength and colour, whereas whole leaf teas take time to unfurl and release their flavour. Some delicate greens may only need a couple of minutes, while black teas usually ask for a little longer to ensure the full flavour is extracted. Oolongs can even need as long as 5 or 6 minutes to allow the leaves to untwist – a process evocatively known in China as "the agony of the leaves". To ensure the best possible cup you'll therefore need to be patient – our historic "dunk and dash" habits won't do whole leaf tea justice but trust us, it'll be worth the wait.

See pages 74–99 to find out the best brewing times for some of our favourite teas.

Milk and Sugar

When customers walk into the Tea Bar and ask for a "breakfast tea", what they really mean is "a tea I can put milk in". Putting milk into the cup, the default setting for Brits, is a habit that can be traced back to the seventeenth and eighteenth centuries when a little milk was poured into fine bone china cups to protect them from the extreme heat of the tea. More recently, when low-quality tea bags proliferated, the proteins in the milk bound to the high levels of bitter tannins in the tea, making for a smoother, more palatable cup. Although many high-quality black teas are best enjoyed without milk, so-called breakfast blends, and their single-origin component parts, such as a malty Assam or a light, bright Ceylon, do undeniably make for a happy marriage with a dash of dairy (semi-skimmed is best – or almond or oat for dairy-free).

Of course, when it comes to the subject of milk and sugar, it is important to remember that it's personal. We've all experienced the office tea round, which is rarely a matter of simply taking numbers, but, instead, lengthy notes detailing how each of your colleagues takes their tea. Similarly, if asked, one can recommend how a particular tea is best enjoyed, but we would be wary of advising anyone unprompted how to take their tea. With that in mind, at the Tea Bar we make milk and sugar readily available for customers so they can do their thing privately.

When it comes to the subject of milk and sugar, it is important to remember that it's personal.

Looking After Your Tea

Tea has a generous shelf life and can last for up to a year, maybe even more – but only if stored correctly. We work hard to get the freshest tea possible from origin, take great care in storing it at our warehouse and then pack it into air-locked, foil-lined pouches to ensure the leaves reach our customers as fresh as possible. But how you store your tea at home will be key to how flavoursome your brew is, and leaves exposed to the elements can lose their oomph, leaving your cup of tea lacking...

In short, the best way to ensure you are always drinking your tea at its best is by storing your tea in a cool, dark, dry place in an airtight container.

WHAT MAKES TEA DETERIORATE?

Deterioration in tea is for the most part caused by oxidation. As soon as tea leaves are picked from the bushes they start to react with oxygen in the air. In fact, for black teas the leaves are bruised after they're picked to actively encourage and speed up this oxidation, resulting in darker, more robust flavours. However, the final stage of production for almost all teas involves the leaves being heated (via steaming, firing or baking) in order to halt that process and ensure the desired flavour profile is "fixed". Correctly storing the finished tea, therefore, ensures that no further oxidation takes place that could alter the flavour of the tea. More delicate, less oxidized teas, such as greens and whites, are naturally the most sensitive to the effects of any ongoing oxidation, while the deterioration of black teas is harder to detect in the cup.

With that in mind, here are a few things to consider when storing your tea, to keep it as fresh and flavoursome as possible:

KEEP IT AIRTIGHT

With exposure to air, or more specifically to oxygen, tea leaves will continue to oxidise. Limit this as far as possible by using an airtight container. The more tea it contains, the less room there is for air to get trapped inside so best to keep the container full.

KEEP IT COOL

Although high heat is used to halt oxidation during tea production, warm temperatures will instead speed up the process. Keeping the teas in a cool place, such as a store cupboard, will therefore reduce the risk of deterioration.

KEEP IT DRY

Adding water to your dry tea leaves is of course what releases flavour when we make a cup of tea. It is therefore important to avoid any contact with moisture until you are ready to brew. Again, for this reason an airtight container stored in a cool, dry place will help keep the tea fresh for longer.

KEEP IT AWAY FROM HERBS AND SPICES

Tea leaves tend to absorb any strong odours around them. We use this quality in the production of Jasmine tea, as the green tea leaves quickly absorb the sweet scent of the jasmine flowers. However, you don't want your black teas to have a minty finish, nor your green teas to taste of cumin, so it's important not only to separate your teas (particularly any heavily scented ones), but to avoid storing them close to your herbs and spices.

DARK IS BEST

Although it is still not clear how exactly light affects the freshness of tea, it does tend to impact flavour and can even leave the tea tasting metallic after a time. Storing your tea in a cupboard away from direct sunlight, or in a dark container, is therefore recommended. Glass is a beautiful way of storing tea and one we use in our Tea Bar to show off the huge variation in leaves, but it is best suited to those teas you drink regularly, so the leaves are not exposed to light for too long. Or even better, put your glass jars in a cupboard.

Some of Our Favourites

Black Tea

ASSAM

Produced in northeast India, in the largest tea-growing region in the world, Assam is the backbone of many breakfast blends. Known as the whisky of the tea world, thanks to its characteristically rich, malty flavour, this much-loved black tea brews a full-bodied, copper-red cup – perfect with a dash of milk.

 Tea leaves   3g (1 rounded teaspoon)/200ml (7fl oz)

 Water temperature   Just boiled

 Brew time   3 minutes

 Origin   Assam, India

FOR THE PERFECT CUP OF ASSAM TEA
Brew 3g (1 rounded teaspoon) of good loose leaves in 200ml (7fl oz) of freshly boiled water for 3 minutes.

DARJEELING

Grown on the steep slopes of the Himalayas, Darjeelings, known as the 'champagne' of teas, are highly sought-after the world over, thanks to their unique, wine-like profile. While the first plucking of the year, or 'first flush', is crisp, floral and delicate, the musky sweetness of the more full-bodied second flush Darjeeling makes for a deliciously fragrant afternoon tea – best enjoyed without milk.

 Tea leaves 3g (1 rounded teaspoon)/200ml (7fl oz)

 Water temperature **Just boiled**

 Brew time **3 minutes**

 Origin **Darjeeling, India**

FOR THE PERFECT CUP OF DARJEELING TEA
Brew 3g (1 rounded teaspoon) of good loose leaves in 200ml (7fl oz) of freshly boiled water for 3 minutes.

CEYLON

Well-loved for its breakfast teas, Sri Lanka has been filling British mugs for over a century. The bright, coppery liquors produced from the leaves grown on this small island are a favourite among milk-and-sugar takers, but are even better black. For a medium-bodied yet aromatic cup, choose a Ceylon grown at a mid–high elevation such as those from Uva or Dimbula.

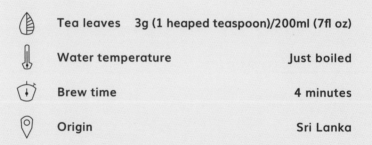

Tea leaves	3g (1 heaped teaspoon)/200ml (7fl oz)	
Water temperature		Just boiled
Brew time		4 minutes
Origin		Sri Lanka

FOR THE PERFECT CUP OF CEYLON TEA
Brew 3g (1 heaped teaspoon) of good loose leaves in 200ml (7fl oz) of freshly boiled water for 4 minutes.

KENYA

From a country best known for producing low-grade CTC (see page 31) comes some of the world's finest black teas. The best of Kenya's orthodox teas (those manufactured using traditional methods) produce deep red liquors and rich, fruity cups with hints of spice – delicious taken with or without milk. If a bold, kickstart-your-day breakfast tea is your thing, Kenyan tea might well be your happy place.

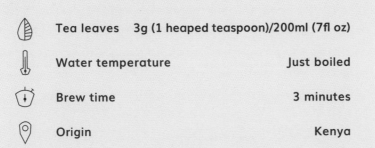

Tea leaves	3g (1 heaped teaspoon)/200ml (7fl oz)	
Water temperature		Just boiled
Brew time		3 minutes
Origin		Kenya

FOR THE PERFECT CUP OF KENYAN TEA
Brew 3g (1 heaped teaspoon) of good loose leaves in 200ml (7fl oz) of freshly boiled water for 3 minutes.

KEEMUN

Grown in the mountainous region of Qimen from which it takes its name, this is one of China's most well-known black teas. The dark leaves produce a deep amber cup, combining a delicately sweet, floral aroma with a lingering cocoa finish. A rich, warming cup for any time of day, this takes milk well but is smooth and fragrant without.

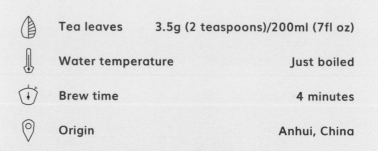

Tea leaves		3.5g (2 teaspoons)/200ml (7fl oz)
Water temperature		Just boiled
Brew time		4 minutes
Origin		Anhui, China

FOR THE PERFECT CUP OF KEEMUN TEA
Brew 3.5g (2 teaspoons) of good loose leaves in 200ml (7fl oz) of freshly boiled water for 4 minutes.

YUNNAN

From one of the oldest and most important tea-growing regions in China, after which it is named, this orthodox black tea typically delivers a delicate smokiness in the aroma, with layers of caramel, cocoa and peppery notes on the finish. Beautiful black for any time of day, Yunnan can also take milk for a rich, malty breakfast tea.

 Tea leaves 3g (1 heaped teaspoon)/200ml (7fl oz)

 Water temperature   **Just boiled**

 Brew time   **3 minutes**

 Origin   **Yunnan, China**

FOR THE PERFECT CUP OF YUNNAN TEA
Brew 3g (1 heaped teaspoon) of good loose leaves in 200ml (7fl oz) of freshly boiled water for 3 minutes.

EARL GREY

Striking a balance between body and aroma, Earl Grey combines a black tea with the heady citrus notes of bergamot. Though traditionally made using a Chinese black tea base, Earl Grey now comes in many guises. Thanks to their natural citrus aroma, Ceylon teas work particularly well, but never has a tea been so divisive, so we encourage you to find the one that is right for you. At its best, Earl Grey makes for a deliciously fragrant cup for any time of day. Delicious with or without milk.

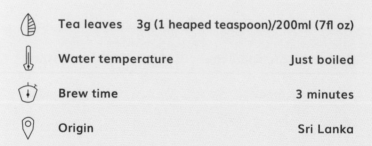

Tea leaves	3g (1 heaped teaspoon)/200ml (7fl oz)	
Water temperature		Just boiled
Brew time		3 minutes
Origin		Sri Lanka

FOR THE PERFECT CUP OF EARL GREY TEA
Brew 3g (1 heaped teaspoon) of good loose leaves in 200ml (7fl oz) of freshly boiled water for 3 minutes.

Oolong

FOUR SEASONS

Grown high in the mountains in Taiwan, where many of the world's best oolongs are produced, the yellow-gold leaves of this lightly oxidized oolong unfurl to produce a fresh, floral cup. Smooth, almost creamy, with lingering notes of tropical fruit, this so-called "Jade" oolong is light, sweet and easygoing for any time of day.

 Tea leaves   2.5g (1 teaspoon)/200ml (7fl oz)

 Water temperature   90°C (195°F)

Brew time   4–6 minutes

Origin   Taiwan

FOR THE PERFECT CUP OF FOUR SEASONS
Brew 2.5g (1 teaspoon) of good loose leaves in 200ml (7fl oz) of 90°C (195°F) water for 4–6 minutes. Good quality leaves can be reinfused multiple times.

IRON BUDDHA (TIE GUAN YIN)

Among the most popular and certainly the best known of the Chinese oolongs, Iron Buddha (also known as Iron Goddess of Mercy) undergoes a medium oxidation and long, careful baking over bamboo. The resulting infusion is honey-sweet and smooth, with notes of roasted chestnuts and dried fruit.

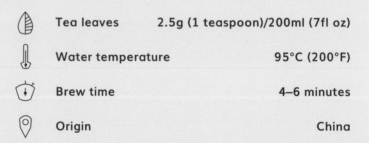

Tea leaves	2.5g (1 teaspoon)/200ml (7fl oz)	
Water temperature		95°C (200°F)
Brew time		4–6 minutes
Origin		China

FOR THE PERFECT CUP OF IRON BUDDHA
Brew 2.5g (1 teaspoon) of good loose leaves in 200ml (7fl oz) of 95°C (200°F) water for 4–6 minutes. Good quality leaves can be reinfused multiple times.

HONEY ORCHID

The most popular of the Phoenix Mountain teas, this dark oolong is named after its particular cultivar, Mi Lan Xiang, meaning "Honey Orchid Fragrance". The infusion should be bursting with orange blossom and apricot, with a toasted, honey-sweet finish produced by the multiple roasts it undergoes.

Tea leaves		2.5g (1 tablespoon)/200ml (7fl oz)
Water temperature		90°C (195°F)
Brew time		4–6 minutes
Origin		China

FOR THE PERFECT CUP OF HONEY ORCHID

Brew 2.5g (1 tablespoon) of good loose leaves in 200ml (7fl oz) of 90°C (195°F) water for 4–6 minutes. Good quality leaves can be reinfused multiple times.

EASTERN BEAUTY (ORIENTAL BEAUTY)

The multi-coloured leaves of this "dark" oolong produce a highly fragrant cup, with hints of orange and caramel. In the Taiwanese summertime, the tea plant is swarmed by green leafhoppers. In self-defence, the plant releases polyphenols and it is this response that gives this tea its distinctive sweet-sour balance and fragrant character.

Tea leaves		2.5g (1 tablespoon)/200ml (7fl oz)
Water temperature		85°C (185°F)
Brew time		4–6 minutes
Origin		Taiwan

FOR THE PERFECT CUP OF EASTERN BEAUTY
Brew 2.5g (1 tablespoon) of good loose leaves in 200ml (7fl oz) of 85°C (185°F) water for 4–6 minutes. Good quality leaves can be reinfused multiple times.

POUCHONG (BAO ZHONG)

The "greenest" and least processed of the oolongs, thanks to minimal oxidation and no roasting, Pouchong retains much of its delicate, floral aroma. With a lingering buttery finish, this makes for a deliciously refreshing afternoon oolong, particularly good on a hot summer's day.

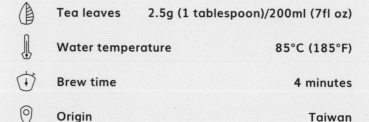

Tea leaves	2.5g (1 tablespoon)/200ml (7fl oz)	
Water temperature		85°C (185°F)
Brew time		4 minutes
Origin		Taiwan

FOR THE PERFECT CUP OF POUCHONG

Brew 2.5g (1 tablespoon) of good loose leaves in 200ml (7fl oz) of 85°C (185°F) water for 4 minutes. Good quality leaves can be reinfused multiple times.

Green Tea

DRAGONWELL / LONG JING

The most famous of China's green teas, originating from Zhejiang province, these spring-green leaves are shaped and fired by hand in hot woks. Not only does this process give them their characteristically flat, sword-like appearance, the pan-firing also lends this green tea its distinctive buttery sweetness and notes of roasted chestnuts.

 Tea leaves   3g (1 heaped teaspoon)/200ml (7fl oz)

 Water temperature   80°C (176°F)

 Brew time   4 minutes

 Origin   China

FOR THE PERFECT CUP OF DRAGONWELL

Brew 3g (1 heaped teaspoon) of good loose leaves in 200ml (7fl oz) of 80°C (176°F) water for 4 minutes. Good quality leaves can be reinfused multiple times.

JADE TIPS / MAO JIAN

Mao Jian translates literally as "fur tips", referring to the tender young leaves that are selected during plucking, consisting of downy buds and long, pointed leaves. Grown and plucked in Xinyang, a unique growing region high in the mountains, this pale green liquor delivers a clean, vegetal aroma with lingering floral sweetness – a deliciously refreshing, everyday green tea.

Tea leaves	2.5g (1 heaped teaspoon)/200ml (7fl oz)	
Water temperature		70°C (158°F)
Brew time		2 minutes
Origin		China

FOR THE PERFECT CUP OF JADE TIPS

Brew 2.5g (1 heaped teaspoon) of good loose leaves in 200ml (7fl oz) of 70°C (158°F) water for 2 minutes. Good quality leaves can be reinfused multiple times.

JASMINE PEARLS

The leaves of this delicate green tea are hand-rolled into a characteristic pearl shape, before being naturally scented with fresh jasmine flowers. The flowers are scattered among the tea leaves at dusk, just as they open and release their heady fragrance. This process may be repeated multiple times to ensure the perfect balance. The result is a deliciously smooth, floral cup for any time of day.

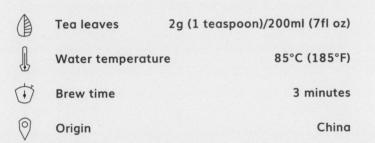

	Tea leaves	2g (1 teaspoon)/200ml (7fl oz)
	Water temperature	85°C (185°F)
	Brew time	3 minutes
	Origin	China

FOR THE PERFECT CUP OF JASMINE PEARLS
Brew 2g (1 teaspoon) of good loose leaves in 200ml (7fl oz) of 85°C (185°F) water for 3 minutes. Good quality leaves can be reinfused multiple times, but the magic of the unfurling pearls will be lost.

MATCHA

This stone-ground green tea has been around for centuries, celebrated for its numerous health benefits, ranging from boosting energy levels, focusing the mind and even speeding up the metabolism. The best is made from the young leaves of the first harvest of the year, which have been shaded for 3–4 weeks before they are picked to bring out sweetness in the cup. Once harvested, the leaves are dried before being ground into a fine powder using a stone or ball mill. The centrepiece of a Japanese tea ceremony, Matcha is traditionally prepared using a bamboo whisk with just hot water and then drunk from a *chawan* or tea bowl, allowing you to sip the tea while also taking in its fresh aroma. Prepared in this traditional way, Matcha should be smooth and creamy, striking a perfect balance between sweet and savoury.

	Water temperature	80°C (176°F)
	Origin	Japan

TO MAKE TRADITIONAL MATCHA
Sift 1.5g or a small teaspoon of Matcha powder into a high-sided bowl. Measure out 80ml (2¾ fl oz) of water at 80°C (176°F) into a small jug. Add a small amount of the water to the powder and mix to make a smooth paste. Add the remaining water and whisk into a fine, creamy foam.

SENCHA

Widely drunk in Japan, Sencha is a steamed green tea typically made from the first spring pickings of the year. The steaming process locks in its bright green colour, after which the tea is dried and rolled to achieve its characteristically long, emerald-green needles. The result is a delicately sweet cup with a fresh, smooth finish, a favourite among green tea aficionados looking for the gentle grassy notes so typical of Japanese teas.

 Tea leaves 3.5g (1 heaped teaspoon)/200ml (7fl oz)

 Water temperature   70°C (158°F)

 Brew time   2 minutes

 Origin   Japan

FOR THE PERFECT CUP OF SENCHA

Brew 3.5g (1 heaped teaspoon) of good loose leaves in 200ml (7fl oz) of 70°C (158°F) water for 2 minutes. Good quality leaves can be reinfused multiple times.

White tea

SILVER NEEDLE
One of the most highly prized teas in the world, these juicy, unopened buds, with their characteristic downy hairs, are hand-picked in Fujian Province, China, the home of white tea, in early spring. The delicate, silky-smooth infusion has a gentle sweetness and a pleasing vegetal aroma.

Tea leaves	4g (1 tablespoon)/200ml (7fl oz)	
Water temperature		80°C (176°F)
Brew time		4 minutes
Origin		China

FOR THE PERFECT CUP OF SILVER NEEDLE
Brew 4g (1 tablespoon) of good loose leaves in 200ml (7fl oz) of 80°C (176°F) water for 4 minutes. Good quality leaves can be reinfused multiple times.

WHITE PEONY

These unopened silver buds and emerald-green leaves are grown and crafted in Fujian Province, China, the home of white tea in China. White Peony produces a delicate, pale gold infusion with notes of honey and melon. Light yet well-rounded and distinctly sweet, this is the perfect introduction to white tea.

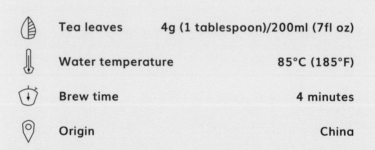

Tea leaves		4g (1 tablespoon)/200ml (7fl oz)
Water temperature		85°C (185°F)
Brew time		4 minutes
Origin		China

FOR THE PERFECT CUP OF WHITE PEONY

Brew 4g (1 tablespoon) of good loose leaves in 200ml (7fl oz) of 85°C (185°F) water for 4 minutes. Good quality leaves can be reinfused multiple times.

Fermented tea

PUER

Puer is an aged and fermented tea, almost exclusively produced in Yunnan province in China and sold in compressed cakes. It is the particular fermentation and ageing process that gives Puer its characteristically earthy and complex flavour, but with some maturing for as long as 30 years, each cake is entirely unique, making the world of Puer tea a treasure trove of flavour to be explored.

Tea leaves		6g (3 teaspoons)/180ml (6fl oz)
Water temperature		Freshly boiled
Brew time		Variable
Origin		China

FOR THE PERFECT CUP OF PUER

First you'll need to break off a section of your cake. Around 6g (3 teaspoons) tea per 180ml freshly boiled water is a good place to start, but you're best experimenting as every Puer is unique. However you choose to brew it, all Puer should be infused multiple times. Much of the joy of drinking this extraordinary tea is experiencing how the flavour evolves across the infusions.

Puer has been designated a protected-origin product. This means that, in order to be called a Puer, the tea must be grown and produced in Yunnan Province in China. Puer teas are so highly prized, in fact, that not only do they fetch a high price tag, but investors the world over will even put serious money behind the future potential of certain teas. The intense, earthy character of a Puer isn't for everyone but these aged teas attract devotees like no other. Just as wine aficionados will hunt down a particular vintage, so tea junkies will delight in getting hold of a Puer.

There is no doubt that its unique ageing process does turn a cup of tea into a product of extraordinary complexity.

DRINKING TEA

Iced Teas

There are few things more refreshing than an iced tea on a hot day and in the summer months we serve it by the gallon. If you have the time, we love cold-brewing for an easy iced tea – see opposite.

For immediate results, however, hot-brewing will also make delicious iced tea of any leaf. If you plan to serve the tea unsweetened, be sure to follow the same brewing instructions you would for your hot tea. While it is tempting to add more tea or extend the brewing time to make up for the strength lost when serving it cold, if you do so you will be left with an unpleasantly bitter cup, which only adding sugar can save.

Cold Brew Tea

You'll need to plan ahead, but tea leaves steeped overnight in cold, filtered water take their time to infuse, making for a smoother, sweeter and more delicate cup. You'll find that many teas are delicious cold-brewed, but teas with aromatic, complex flavour profiles, such as oolongs or Darjeeling, have particularly delicious results.

MAKES 1 LITRE

6–10g or 1 heaped tablespoon of tea leaves of your choice (see note below)

1 litre (1¾ pints) cold filtered water

Simply steep the tea in cold, filtered water for 12–15 hours in the fridge. Every tea will perform a little differently but it's hard to go too far wrong with cold-brewing, so experiment a little with your time and ratios.

Once happy with the taste, strain the leaves and keep it in the fridge for 2 days.

Note: white teas and herbs aren't heated during processing, so be sure to give them a quick 'wash' with boiling water before infusing to kill any bacteria.

Traditional Iced Tea

There is a very good reason why every household in America has a jug of iced tea in their fridge. Iced tea in any form can rehydrate and revive like nothing else, and it couldn't be simpler to make. The following recipe makes two tall glasses, but it may well be worth scaling this up once or twice so that you too can have a jug on hand at any time of day or night.

MAKES 2 TALL GLASSES
Ice
4 slices of lemon
5g or 2 heaped teaspoons of Ceylon tea leaves
½ teaspoon honey

Fill a large jug with plenty of ice and a couple of lemon slices. Similarly prepare two tall glasses with ice and a slice of lemon in each.

Measure out the tea leaves into a heatproof jug or teapot and pour over 300ml (10fl oz) of freshly boiled water. Steep for 5 minutes, then strain the leaves. Stir in the honey and pour over the ice in the jug.

Muddle frantically until the jug feels cold to the touch. The idea here is to let the ice chill the tea, but not for the ice cubes to melt, so it's important to keep the liquid moving!

Pour your tea into the prepared glasses and enjoy.

Ceylon tea is particularly well suited to this recipe thanks to its bright citrus notes, but any black tea will do.

Arnold Palmer

This iced tea is named after a golfer who, in the fifties, reportedly created this drink as his preferred refreshment after a round. The simple yet particularly refreshing combination of iced tea and lemonade has since adopted his name. Here we suggest a twist on tradition by choosing either a rich, chocolatey Keemun black tea as your base or a lighter, more fragrant Jasmine tea. It is worth noting that an Arnold Palmer is unapologetically a sweetened iced tea. If you would prefer to ease off the sugar, by all means do so.

As with many of these iced teas, you may well want to consume the tea in larger quantities than one or two glasses, so feel free to scale up the recipe for a jug. Pictured on page 111.

MAKES 2 TALL GLASSES
Ice
5g or 2 teaspoons Keemun or Jasmine tea leaves
2 tablespoons sugar
Juice of ½ lemon
100ml (3½ fl oz) soda water

Prepare two tall glasses with plenty of ice.

Measure out the tea into a heatproof jug or teapot and pour over 300ml (10fl oz) of freshly boiled water. Brew for 5 minutes, then strain the liquor into a separate jug and stir the sugar into the warm tea. Add the lemon juice and plenty of ice, muddling quickly until the jug is cold to the touch.

Divide between the two prepared glasses and top up with soda water.

Hibiscus Fizz

You won't find many Hibiscus iced teas being served in cafés in western societies, yet elsewhere in the world hibiscus flowers are brewed with merriment. Barely a meal passes in Mexico without a jug of so-called "Agua de Jamaica" waiting nearby. Hibiscus flowers, when steeped in boiling water, produce a fruity yet devilishly tart herbal infusion Sometimes known as "sour tea", its flavour is often likened to the sharp acidity of a cranberry. Here we've softened the tang with a little brown sugar, making this deep red creation a wonderful refreshment for a hot day. Pictured on page 110.

MAKES 2 TALL GLASSES
Ice
2 slices of lime
3g or 1 heaped teaspoon of
  Hibiscus leaves
½ teaspoon brown sugar
150ml(5fl oz) sparkling water

Prepare two glasses with plenty of ice and a slice of lime in each.

Prepare a Hibiscus concentrate by steeping the Hibiscus leaves in 100ml (3½fl oz) of freshly drawn and boiled water for 5 minutes. Strain the liquor, add the sugar into the warm tea and stir well to dissolve. Pour the sweetened Hibiscus concentrate over ice in the prepared glasses and muddle to chill.

Top up with cold sparkling water, and extra ice if needed, and drink immediately.

You may well want to prepare plenty of this tea in the summer months. If so, a large batch of the sweetened hibiscus concentrate, perhaps five times this recipe, can be made and stored in the fridge in an airtight bottle for up to a week. To drink, simply pour the liquor over ice and lime slices and top up with sparkling water in the same ratio as in the recipe.

HIBISCUS FIZZ

ARNOLD PALMER

Darjeeling & Elderflower Cold Brew

A Good & Proper staple, this iced tea is the ultimate refreshment and one we serve by the gallon from the van every year to parched festival-goers on hot summer days. It's painfully simple and loved by all, yet the addition of Darjeeling – the champagne of teas – makes for an elegant twist. Pictured on page 114.

MAKES 2 TALL GLASSES

3g or 1 heaped teaspoon of Darjeeling tea leaves

500ml (18fl oz) cold, filtered water

50ml (2fl oz) elderflower cordial

Ice

In order to achieve both the most vibrant colour in the glass and the most complex flavour, we recommend cold-brewing the Darjeeling overnight. Weigh out the tea into a bottle or jug and add 500ml (18fl oz) of cold, filtered water. Cover or secure the lid on the bottle and place in the fridge overnight (or for around 12–15 hours). The following day, strain the tea, discarding the leaves, and return the tea to its bottle where it will sit happily in the fridge for 3 days.

When you are ready to drink it, put 25ml (¾fl oz) of elderflower cordial in each glass and add plenty of ice. Pour over your cold-brewed tea and muddle to combine.

Here are some other easy cold-brews, all of them unsweetened:

If you want to brew this and drink it straight away, measure out the tea and cover with freshly drawn and boiled water. Steep for 5 minutes, strain and then pour over ice. Muddle with a spoon until the tea is cold, then add this tea to your elderflower syrup and ice as before and enjoy.

ROOIBOS & ORANGE
Rinse 6g or 4 teaspoons of Rooibos tea leaves with boiling water before adding to 500ml (18fl oz) cold, filtered water to brew overnight in the fridge. Taste to test, strain and serve with ice and a slice of orange.

WHITE PEONY & PEAR
Rinse 3g or 2 heaped teaspoons of White Peony tea leaves with boiling water before adding to 500ml (18fl oz) cold, filtered water to brew overnight in the fridge. Taste to test, strain and serve with ice and a slice of pear.

LEMON VERBENA & FRESH MINT
Rinse 3g or 3 tablespoons of Lemon Verbena tea leaves with boiling water before adding to 500ml (18fl oz) cold, filtered water to brew overnight in the fridge. Taste to test, strain and serve with ice and fresh mint.

Iced Green Tea & Apple

The savoury, vegetal notes of a green tea can be divisive, but when chilled and combined with the tart freshness of a crisp green apple, it is a whole new drink. Here we use Jade Tips, or Mao Jian, a deliciously refreshing Chinese green tea that will appeal to fans and new adopters alike. Its clean flavour and delicate sweetness is brought to life by the addition of the green apple and a little sugar.

It is worth noting that to get the best flavour from green tea, you want to avoid brewing with boiling water – about 75°C (167°F) is ideal. This can be achieved by either flipping the lid of the kettle once boiled and leaving the water for a couple of minutes to cool, or pouring the water into a separate pot and adding a splash of cold. See page 62 for more about brewing temperatures. Pictured on page 119.

MAKES 2 TALL GLASSES

¼ Granny Smith apple, cored and cut into thin slices

5g or 1 heaped teaspoon soft brown sugar

Ice

5g or 2 teaspoons of Jade Tips green tea leaves

Place the apple slices and sugar in a jug and set aside. Prepare two glasses with plenty of ice and an extra slice of apple in each.

Steep the green tea leaves for 5 minutes in 200ml (7fl oz) of cooled boiled water. Strain and pour the tea into the jug and stir to dissolve the sugar. When dissolved, add plenty of ice to the jug and muddle vigorously to chill the tea. Strain again to remove the steeped apple slices, then pour the chilled tea into your prepared glasses.

DARJEELING &
ELDERFLOWER

LEMON VERBENA &
FRESH MINT

WHITE PEONY
& PEAR

ROOIBOS
& ORANGE

Ruby Red

This particular iced tea is the creation of a lovely barista, Emily with a 'y', who we had the privilege of employing at Good & Proper Tea when we first opened our London Tea Bar. Our Ruby Oolong, with its tightly rolled leaves, is a heavily fermented oolong that has been slowly baked to bring out the rich flavours of cacao, raisins and black cherry. Those flavours are lifted by the acidity and sweetness of the pink grapefruit here to make a unique and deliciously refreshing iced tea. Pictured on page 118.

MAKES 2 TALL GLASSES
3g or 1 teaspoon of Ruby
Oolong tea leaves
Ice
1 grapefruit, juiced
Grapefruit slices, to garnish
(optional)

This iced tea is at its best cold-brewed, so you'll need to prepare your Ruby Oolong cold brew in advance. As this is a tightly rolled oolong, it pays to rinse the tea briefly in boiling water before infusing to "wake up" the leaves. Then add your tea leaves to a bottle or jug and add 500ml (18fl oz) of cold, filtered water. Cover or secure the lid on the bottle and place in the fridge overnight (or for around 12–15 hours). The following day, strain the tea, discarding the leaves, and return the tea to its bottle where it will sit happily in the fridge for 3 days. With your cold brew now at the ready, making the finished drink couldn't be easier.

Prepare two glasses with plenty of ice. Add half the grapefruit juice to each glass and top up with Ruby Oolong cold brew. Stir to combine and chill, garnish with a slice of grapefruit and enjoy.

If tempted, you can turn this into a simple but addictive apéritif-style cocktail by adding a shot of Aperol or Campari to each glass.

Yunnan, Orange & Ginger Iced Tea

This is perhaps the most surprising and addictive of all of our iced teas and one we've turned to time and time again since our first manager, the lovable Aussie Ashleigh, made it for us one sunny day many years ago. Even now, having made hundreds of them, we are still surprised at the effect the Yunnan has on the drink. Smoky and complex, this can be a thirst-quenching soft drink for any time of day, but it comes into its own served as an alternative to a cocktail for those avoiding alcohol. Having said that, a wee drop of whisky also makes for a delicious addition. As before, feel free to scale up the recipe for a jugful. We guarantee it will all be drunk. Pictured on page 118.

MAKES 2 TALL GLASSES
Ice
2 slices of orange
5g or 2 heaped teaspoons of
  Yunnan tea leaves
Ginger ale

Prepare two glasses with plenty of ice and an orange slice in each.

Measure out the tea leaves into a heatproof jug or teapot and pour over 300ml (10fl oz) of freshly boiled water. Steep for 5 minutes before straining into a separate jug filled with ice. Muddle frantically until the jug feels cold to the touch.

Fill your prepared glasses two-thirds full with tea and top up the remaining third with ginger ale.

YUNNAN, ORANGE
& GINGER ICED TEA

RUBY RED

ICED GREEN TEA
& APPLE

Tea Lattes

Not just the domain of espresso, some teas also stand up well to a heavy dose of milk and, as such, can be served as a warming tea latte. Matcha's pop of bright green looks and tastes amazing in perfectly steamed milk, while we use our Lemongrass to add a zing to a turmeric latte. Tea lattes are not just for winter, either, with a glass full of ice turning any of them into a summertime staple.

When making lattes at home, a little trick will make for a smoother, creamier finish. If you've got a French press or cafetière, simply add your hot milk and plunge enthusiastically up and down until the milk has doubled in volume. Just make sure you get rid of any residual coffee aromas before you begin!

Coconut Matcha Latte

We didn't always serve Matcha lattes at the Tea Bar, the purist in me believing them to be a novelty drink on a par with pumpkin-spiced lattes and other overly sweetened hot drinks I so keenly avoid. I would still urge tea lovers to try a Traditional Matcha (see page 92) first, to fully appreciate the uniquely heady aroma of this exquisite green tea. However, Matcha lattes seem to inhabit a neat, happy place between tea and coffee, the addition of milk making it a deliciously creamy alternative to your morning flat white – and indeed one with all of the caffeine, without the jitters.

Playing around with dairy-free recipes before an event, we were delighted with the results of this particular creation. The natural sweetness of the coconut milk perfectly balances the savoury notes of the Matcha, and it is now one of our bestsellers at the Tea Bar. For a traditional Matcha, you would ideally have a bamboo Matcha whisk and tea bowl, or chawan, but for a latte just a wide coffee cup and simple whisk will do.

If you don't have a temperature-controlled kettle, to get water at 60°C (140°F), simply boil the kettle and allow to stand for 5 minutes with the lid open or mix freshly boiled water with cold water at a ratio of 1:4 cold to boiling. See page 62 for more on brewing temperatures.

MAKES 2 CUPS

1 teaspoon Matcha tea powder, sifted

20ml or 4 teaspoons hot water (about 60°C (140°F); see tip)

240ml (8½ fl oz) unsweetened coconut milk

½ teaspoon honey

Put your sifted Matcha powder into the base of your cup and add the hot water. Use a whisk to make a smooth, green paste in the base of your cup, making sure you get rid of any lumps.

Heat the coconut milk and honey in a small saucepan over a medium heat until it starts to steam and is just shy of a simmer. You can pour this over the Matcha shot straight away if you like, but for the full effect, pour your milk into a cafetière and plunge enthusiastically up and down until the milk has doubled in volume, giving you a perfectly frothed latte.

To finish, slowly pour the milk through the Matcha shot, stir gently to combine and enjoy.

Masala Chai Spice Mix

This spiced and sweetened milky tea is the elixir on which much of India fuels itself. If you've ever had the pleasure, you will recognize the heady spicing and immediately be transported back. The street vendors, accustomed to making this tea all day long, make it look painfully easy, with palmfuls of tea leaves, pinches of spice and sprinkles of sugar flamboyantly chucked into their large pans, ensuring that no two cups taste the same. To make this at home, we've given you two options. Below we have listed the recipe for a large batch of Chai spice mix that, stored in an airtight container, will take you through plenty of cups of Chai whenever you fancy. Alternatively, see page 128 for a recipe for small quantities of Chai for immediate consumption.

**MAKES ENOUGH FOR
5–6 TEAS**

**10g (2 teaspoons)
cardamom pods**

30g (1oz) cinnamon stick

**10g (2 teaspoons) ground
ginger**

5g (1 teaspoon) cloves

**10g (2 teaspoons) whole black
peppercorns**

Rich, malty Assam tea works particularly well with Chai, but if you don't have any to hand, any strong black tea will do. For a dairy-free option, oat milk works best.

Weigh out all the spices and combine using a pestle and mortar or spice grinder. You do not want to break these spices to a powder, so pound or pulse them until they are broken down but still visible as shards and scraps. Decant the mix to an airtight container and store in a cool, dark place until ready to use. The spice mix will last, properly sealed, for up to 3 months.

To prepare two Chai lattes, add 2 heaped teaspoons of your Chai spice mix and 2 teaspoons (5g) Assam black tea to 240ml (8½fl oz) milk and 1½ teaspoons light brown sugar. Combine these ingredients in a saucepan and place over a medium heat. Bring to the boil, taking care the milk doesn't boil over, then reduce the heat to a low simmer and steep for 5 minutes, stirring occasionally.

You can, of course, drink the latte as it is. For the full effect, however, simply pour your Chai into a cafetière and plunge enthusiastically up and down until it has doubled in volume, giving you a perfectly frothed latte. Divide between two cups and enjoy.

Quick Masala Chai Latte

This quick recipe is perfect for when you want to prepare just two cups of Chai for immediate consumption, made by adding a small amount of whole spices directly to the milk. For a caffeine-free twist, you can replace the Assam tea with Rooibos to make a Rooibos Chai (see tip).

MAKES 2 CUPS

2.5cm (1 inch) cinnamon stick

4 cardamom pods

½ teaspoon ground ginger

1 clove

4 whole black peppercorns

2 teaspoons Assam tea leaves

240ml (8½ fl oz) milk

1½ teaspoons light brown sugar

Combine all the ingredients in a saucepan and place over a medium heat. Bring to the boil, taking care the milk doesn't boil over, then reduce the heat to a low simmer. Steep for 5 minutes, stirring occasionally, then strain.

You can, of course, drink the latte as it is. For the full effect, however, simply pour your Chai into a cafetière and plunge enthusiastically up and down until your milk has doubled in volume, giving you a perfectly frothed latte. Divide between two cups and enjoy.

If you make this with Rooibos, you might want to substitute the brown sugar for maple syrup and add a twist of orange peel if you are feeling especially indulgent.

Turmeric & Lemongrass Latte

This heady drink is a multi-sensory experience. The so-called 'sunshine latte' has gained popularity of late, thanks to the alleged health benefits of the turmeric, ginger and cayenne combination, but for us it's just delicious. We've added Lemongrass for a sweet, lemon-sherbet twist, equally enjoyable hot in the winter or over ice in the summer. Pictured on page 130.

MAKES 2 CUPS

2.5cm (1 inch) piece of fresh root ginger, peeled and grated

2.5cm (1 inch) piece of fresh root turmeric, peeled and grated (or ¼ teaspoon ground turmeric if fresh turmeric is tricky to find)

2 pinches of cayenne pepper

2g or 2 teaspoons Lemongrass herbal tea leaves

240ml (8½ fl oz) unsweetened coconut milk

1 teaspoon honey or agave

Ground cinnamon, to serve (optional)

Combine all the ingredients except the cinnamon in a saucepan and place over a medium heat. Bring to the boil, taking care the milk doesn't boil over, then reduce to a low simmer and steep for 4 minutes. You may want to stir the latte occasionally to incorporate all the spices into the milk.

You can, of course, drink the latte as it is. For the full effect, however, simply pour the mixture into a cafetière and plunge enthusiastically up and down until it has doubled in volume, giving you a perfectly frothed latte. Divide between two cups, top each cup with a pinch of cinnamon, if you like, and enjoy immediately.

If it is hot outside but you are still craving this latte, simply pour it over plenty of ice.

Hojicha & Vanilla Latte

Perhaps the most unusual of our tea lattes and one only really seen served in Japan, this is also one of my favourites. Unlike other green teas, Hojicha is roasted after production, lending this latte a honey caramel note that is picked up by the natural sweetness of the maple syrup and vanilla. Hojicha is lower in caffeine than other green teas, making this a latte for comfort more than pick-me-up, and its sweet maltiness has an immediately calming, almost soporific, effect. Pictured on page 135.

MAKES 2 CUPS

4g or 2 level teaspoons Hojicha green tea leaves

240ml (8½ fl oz) oat milk

¼ teaspoon maple syrup

¼ teaspoon vanilla extract

Ground cinnamon or cocoa powder, to serve (optional)

Measure 60ml (4 tablespoons) of freshly boiled water into a heatproof mug or jug and add the tea leaves. Allow to steep for 4 minutes before straining and setting aside the liquor while you prepare the milk.

Put the oat milk in a small pan over a medium heat and bring to the boil. Remove the pan from the heat, add the Hojicha liquor, maple syrup and vanilla and stir to combine. Taste to check the levels of sweetness, adjusting the amount of maple syrup and vanilla to your preference.

You can, of course, drink the latte as it is. For the full effect, however, simply pour the mixture into a cafetière and plunge enthusiastically up and down until it has doubled in volume, giving you a perfectly frothed latte. Divide between two cups and feel free to dust the latte with a little cinnamon or cocoa before drinking.

Rooibos Latte

While somewhat of a novelty in the UK and elsewhere, "red lattes" are found on most coffee-shop menus in South Africa, the native home of Rooibos, or "red bush" tea. Now a firm favourite at the Tea Bar (and often hunted down by homesick South Africans!), this simple winter drink is naturally sweet, velvety smooth and delightfully caffeine-free. We think it works best made with the creamy texture of oat milk, but it's just as happy with full-fat dairy milk. Pictured on page 135.

MAKES 2 CUPS

4g or 2 teaspoons Rooibos tea leaves

240ml (8½ fl oz) oat milk

¼ teaspoon honey

Combine the Rooibos and milk in a small saucepan and place over a medium heat. Bring slowly to the boil, then turn off the heat. Leave the Rooibos to steep for 4 minutes before straining out the leaves. Add the honey to the warm mixture and stir to dissolve. Taste to check the levels of sweetness, adjusting the honey to your preference.

You can, of course, drink the latte as it is. For the full effect, however, simply pour the mixture into a cafetière and plunge enthusiastically up and down until it has doubled in volume, giving you a perfectly frothed latte.

ROOIBOS
LATTE

HOJICHA &
VANILLA LATTE

Cocktails

Earl Grey Sour

Cocktail bartenders love tea. Thanks to the endless varieties, each with its distinct flavour profile and character, tea is the perfect aromatic to lift an existing recipe, or even to take centre stage and balance the other ingredients around. The ever-popular Earl Grey, with its heady bergamot aroma, is always a winner in both cocktails and iced teas, lending citrus and peppery notes to a drink. You need to infuse the gin with Earl Grey tea leaves for 4 hours before making this cocktail.

MAKES 2 COUPE GLASSES

2.5g or 1 heaped teaspoon Earl Grey tea leaves

100ml (3½fl oz) gin

50ml (2fl oz) freshly squeezed lemon juice

2 medium egg whites

50ml (2fl oz) sugar syrup (see page 141)

Ice

Add the Earl Grey tea to the gin and leave to infuse for 4 hours. Strain before using. (It might be worth making a sizeable batch of infused gin if this is a cocktail you think you might make often.)

Chill 2 coupe glasses in the freezer while you prepare the drinks.

For the cocktail, simply pour the infused gin and the rest of the ingredients, except the ice, into a cocktail shaker. Give it a good shake to ensure an even mix. Add plenty of ice and shake vigorously until the outside of the shaker feels ice-cold.

Strain the cocktail through a small sieve into the chilled glasses and enjoy.

Green Tea & Pear Mar-tea-ni

If a well-mixed martini is the hallmark of any good bartender, this concoction will make mixologists of us all. You'll need to prepare the infused vodka ahead of time, but otherwise this is a simple drink to make and an equally simple drink to consume. Given its strength – one part eau de vie and four parts vodka – caution should be taken when drinking. Pictured on page 143.

MAKES 2 MARTINIS
100ml (3½ fl oz) vodka
4g or 2 teaspoons green tea
  leaves
25ml (5 teaspoons)
  Poire Williams
20ml (4 teaspoons) lemon juice
20ml (4 teaspoons) apple juice
Ice
Thin slices of fresh pear,
  to garnish

Begin by infusing your vodka with the green tea. This should be left to infuse for at least an hour, but anywhere up to 4 hours is ideal.

Chill two martini glasses in the freezer whilst you prepare the drinks.

To mix the drink, simply combine the ice-infused vodka, Poire, lemon juice and apple juice in a cocktail shaker and shake, vigorously, until the outside of the shaker feels ice-cold.

Strain into the chilled martini glasses, add your garnishes and enjoy. Repeat as necessary, but perhaps no more than twice in an evening...

A grassy Japanese Sencha works best here thanks to the intense, vegetal character, but if not available, any green tea will do.

Chamomile Gin Fizz

A botanic gin lifted by the sweet vanilla notes of Chamomile is a lovely thing. For those after a light and refreshing gin-based cocktail this offers something delicious and a little different. Pictured on page 142.

MAKES 2 SHORT DRINKS

30ml (1fl oz) sugar syrup (see below)

1 Chamomile tea bag or 1.5g/1 heaped teaspoon of Chamomile flowers

90ml (3fl oz) gin

50ml (2fl oz) lemon juice

60ml (2½fl oz) egg white (2 medium egg whites)

Ice

50ml (2fl oz) soda water

Chamomile flowers (optional), to garnish

FOR THE SUGAR SYRUP (ENOUGH FOR A BATCH)

100g (3½oz) caster sugar

100ml (3½fl oz) boiling water

Begin by making the sugar syrup. This can be done in a batch as it keeps for eternity. Simply put an equal weight of sugar and water (we would suggest 100g (3½oz) sugar and 100ml (3½fl oz) water) in a pan and warm over a medium heat. As soon as the sugar dissolves, remove from the heat and allow to cool.

Prepare your Chamomile tea by brewing the Chamomile in 100ml (3½fl oz) of freshly boiled water for 5 minutes.

While the tea brews, prepare two short glasses with plenty of ice.

Dry shake (meaning without ice) the sugar syrup, gin, lemon juice and egg white in a cocktail shaker. Once brewed, strain the Chamomile tea into the shaker and add plenty of ice, then shake vigorously for 2 minutes. This will whip the egg white, giving you a deliciously frothy cocktail.

Strain the cocktail into the prepared glasses, top up with soda water, and if you want to go all out, garnish with Chamomile flowers.

OOLONG
MOJITO

CHAMOMILE
GIN FIZZ

GREEN TEA & PEAR
MAR-TEA-NI

Oolong Mojito

This will stand up to any mojito you've had before. In fact, the addition of the Four Seasons Oolong, with its smooth floral notes and hints of tropical fruit, brings a whole new dimension to this much-loved drink. Pictured on page 142.

MAKES 2 TALL GLASSES
10g (4 teaspoons) Four
    Seasons Oolong tea leaves
Ice
6 mint sprigs, leaves picked
4 teaspoons brown sugar
Juice of 1½ limes
90ml (3fl oz) white rum

Start by preparing your oolong tea. Bring freshly drawn water to the boil, then leave it for a few minutes to cool. Measure out your tea leaves into a teapot or heatproof jug, add 400ml (14fl oz) of your hot water, and steep for 5 minutes. Strain, then set the liquor aside to cool.

Prepare two tall glasses with plenty of ice.

Add the mint, sugar and lime juice to a cocktail shaker or large jug and muddle together vigorously. Add the rum, the cooled oolong and plenty of ice. Muddle or shake again and taste, adjusting the lime or sugar to your taste. Strain into the prepared glasses and enjoy.

Mandarin Sling

This exquisite drink is the creation of friend and cocktail-craftsman Sam, aka The Rum Runner, who made it for the launch party of our Leather Lane Tea Bar back in 2015. It would be hard to replicate the moment when friends, family and journalists first set foot in our jewellery-warehouse-turned-Tea Bar to mark the start of an exciting new chapter. As a result this cocktail, served by Sam and his team dressed in bow ties, has never tasted better. Nonetheless, it is most certainly a recipe worth sharing, with the citrus of the mandarin cutting perfectly through the grassy Sencha green tea for an incredibly refreshing drink. Definitely one to impress. Pictured on page 147.

MAKES 2 SHORT DRINKS

1g or ½ teaspoon Sencha tea leaves

Ice

50ml (2fl oz) vodka

20ml (4 teaspoons) lime juice

10ml (2 teaspoons) agave syrup

Juice of ½ mandarin

2 mint sprigs, plus extra to garnish

2 dashes of cardamom bitters

Start by preparing your green tea. Bring freshly drawn water to a boil then leave it for a good five minutes to cool slightly. Measure out your tea leaves into a teapot or heatproof jug, add 50ml (3½fl oz) of your hot water and steep for 4 minutes. Strain, then set the liquor aside to cool.

Prepare two short glasses with plenty of ice.

Having made the green tea, this is sinfully simple to make. Add all the ingredients to a cocktail shaker or jug. Add ice and shake or muddle well. Divide between the two prepared glasses and enjoy.

Hibiscus Margarita

This Señorita is a favourite of ours for events, the bright pink colour making it particularly enticing. Be warned, that tequila can really sneak up on you.

To serve this the Mexican way, dip the rim of the glasses first in lime juice then in salt or powdered chilli. Smoked salt has a lovely flavour, if you can get your hands on it.

MAKES 2 SHORT DRINKS
3g or 1 heaped teaspoon of Hibiscus leaves
Juice of 1 lime (keep the squeezed-out halves)
1 tablespoon smoked salt for the rim (if not possible, use a nice sea salt ground together in a pestle and mortar with ½ teaspoon of chilli powder)
60ml (2fl oz) tequila
15ml (½ fl oz) agave syrup
Ice
2 slices of lime

Measure out the Hibiscus leaves into a teapot or heatproof jug. Steep in 50ml (2fl oz) of freshly boiled water for 6 minutes. Strain the liquor and leave to one side to cool.

Prepare two glasses by rubbing their rims with the squeezed-out lime halves and then dipping the rims in the smoked salt.

Add the tequila, lime juice, agave syrup and the cooled Hibiscus tea to a cocktail shaker or jug. Add plenty of ice and shake or muddle well.

Divide the margarita between the two prepared glasses, garnish each with a slice of lime and enjoy.

MANDARIN
SLING

HIBISCUS
MARGARITA

Chai Bourbon Mule

*Smoky, heady with spice and not too sweet, this is a drink that is
so much more than the sum of its parts.*

MAKES 2 TALL GLASSES
Ice
2 slices of lime
**2.5g or 1 heaped teaspoon
  Assam tea leaves**
7.5cm (3 inch) cinnamon stick
**2 cardamom pods, bashed to
  open slightly**
**90ml (3fl oz) bourbon or
  whisky**
Juice of 1 lime
300ml (10fl oz) ginger ale

Prepare two whisky glasses with plenty of ice and a slice of lime
in each.

Measure the tea leaves, cinnamon stick and cardamom pods into a
mug or heatproof jug and cover with 100ml (3½fl oz) of freshly boiled
water. Leave to steep for 5 minutes before straining the liquor and
discarding the spices and tea.

Add the bourbon, lime juice and infused tea to a jug or cocktail shaker,
and muddle or shake to combine. Add plenty of ice and shake or
muddle vigorously. Strain the drink into the two prepared glasses,
top up with ginger ale and enjoy.

Pink Grapefruit, Fennel & Lemon Verbena Gimlet

The Gimlet is a gin-based cocktail and this version of ours is a very strong one. The combination of the sharp grapefruit, the warm spice of the fennel and the smooth lemonyness of the Lemon Verbena may mask its strength, but be warned, it packs a real punch.

MAKES 2 SHORT DRINKS
Ice
50ml (2fl oz) pink grapefruit
   juice or the freshly squeezed
   juice from ½ pink grapefruit
50ml (2fl oz) Fennel & Lemon
   Verbena Syrup (see below)
50ml (2fl oz) gin

**FOR THE FENNEL & LEMON
   VERBENA SYRUP**
2g or 2 tablespoons Lemon
   Verbena leaves
1 teaspoon fennel seeds, plus
   extra to garnish
50ml (2fl oz) water
50g (2oz) caster sugar

Begin by making the syrup. Put all the ingredients in a small saucepan and warm over a medium heat until the sugar is dissolved. Remove from the heat and leave to steep for 5 minutes.

Prepare two short glasses with plenty of ice.

Put the grapefruit juice, cooled syrup (don't worry about the seeds and leaves, they are good for flavour and will be strained out eventually), and gin into a cocktail shaker filled with plenty of ice. Shake for about 20 seconds. Strain into the two prepared glasses and garnish with a few fennel seeds.

COOKING WITH TEA

Baking with Tea

Good & Proper Crumpets

OK, so these don't actually feature tea, but having become somewhat of a Good & Proper staple and one that is uniquely delicious with a cup of tea, we couldn't resist featuring the recipe. A true labour of love, we've been tweaking and evolving this recipe since we first served them at our Old Street Kiosk in 2014, the use of sourdough elevating this pillowy breakfast staple to a new, more flavoursome level. Good & Proper crumpets are now served by the thousand from both our Leather Lane Tea Bar and Watson the Tea Van at festivals throughout the summer. We even feature a monthly Crumpet Collaboration on our menu, with a different chef taking the stage each time to show off their crumpet-based creativity. Once you've mastered the crumpets themselves with the below recipe, it'll be over to you to get creating, and trust us, the opportunities, both sweet and savoury, are endless.

Note: You will need a lively sourdough starter for these crumpets. If you don't have a sourdough starter, you may well be able to beg a small amount from a friend. You can then add equal parts of flour and water to make your own. If you want to get your own sourdough starter going, simply search the internet for sourdough starter recipes and there will be page after page of recipes and instructions. It'll then be down to you to keep your new pet sourdough starter alive by removing half the starter each day and replacing it with the same weight in flour and water in a 50:50 ratio.

These crumpets freeze well once cooked and can be defrosted and toasted when you want them.

(continued on page 158)

Good & Proper Crumpets
(continued)

MAKES 8–10 CRUMPETS
STAGE 1: THE LEVAIN
30g (1oz) sourdough starter
  (see introduction)
110ml (3½ fl oz) cold water
110g (3½ oz) strong white
  flour

STAGE 2: THE CRUMPETS
1 tablespoon caster sugar
300ml (½ pint) whole milk
250ml (9fl oz) hot water
250g (9oz) levain (made in
  Stage 1)
200g (7oz) plain flour
200g (7oz) strong white flour
250ml (9fl oz) cold water
1 tablespoon bicarbonate
  of soda
2 teaspoons fine sea salt
Sunflower oil, for greasing

To cook the crumpets, you
  will need metal rings
  approximately 8.5cm (3½
  in) across (either round or
  square) to achieve a good
  shape

On the morning of your crumpet-making day, mix 30g (1oz) of your sourdough starter (from the half that you are discarding that day) with the water and strong white flour in a mixing bowl until smooth. Leave covered in a warm place for at least an hour, ideally two, which will create your levain.

When your levain is ready, bubbling and lively, measure out the sugar, milk and hot water into a large mixing bowl and whisk to combine. Add your levain and mix well to a batter.

Sift the two flours into a separate bowl then add into the batter, little by little, whisking to avoid lumps. Intermittently scrape down the sides and keep whisking until you have a nice smooth batter. Cover with a clean cloth and leave to prove for 45 minutes to 1 hour. A few bubbles should start to form on top, if not give the batter a bit more time, checking again after a further 15 minutes.

Once the batter is proved, mix together the cold water, bicarbonate of soda and salt in another bowl. Stir to combine and then stir this through the batter. It should start to rise immediately. Cover the batter again and leave to prove for a final 20–30 minutes.

Grease the rings with sunflower oil and place in a heavy-bottomed frying pan over a medium heat. Add a small ladleful (120ml/4fl oz) of batter to each ring. Cook for 12 minutes without moving or turning. Keep an eye on the batter and note the air bubbles forming in the batter as it cooks. The crumpets are ready to be turned when the surface is full of bubbles and just set on top. At this point, carefully remove the rings and flip the crumpets to sear the other side for about 10 seconds before transferring them to a cooling rack. Oil the rings again and repeat until all batter is used and you have a healthy pile of crumpets ready for cold butter and a cup of tea.

Earl Grey & Lemon Drizzle Cake

This is a classic lemon drizzle cake, given a twist by the aromatic notes of the bergamot and gentle astringency of Earl Grey tea. It is the final touch that you never knew your lemon drizzle cake needed.

MAKES A 900G (2LB) CAKE
150ml (¼ pint) buttermilk
20g (3/4oz) or 10 teaspoons of Earl Grey tea leaves
2 eggs, separated
60ml (4 tablespoons) sunflower oil, plus extra for greasing
½ teaspoon vanilla essence
150g (5½ oz) plain flour
3 teaspoons baking powder
190g (6½ oz) caster sugar
¼ teaspoon bicarbonate of soda
2 lemons, zested

Preheat the oven to 170°C/340°F/Gas Mark 3½ and grease and line a 23cm (9 inch) cake tin with baking paper.

Put the buttermilk and tea leaves in a small saucepan over a medium heat, bring gently to a simmer, simmer for 3 minutes and then set aside to cool.

Once cool, strain the buttermilk into a mixing bowl but don't discard the tea leaves.

Put the egg yolks into the bowl with the cooled buttermilk, add the oil and vanilla and whisk until incorporated. In a separate bowl, whisk the egg whites to stiff peaks.

Add the dry ingredients and the lemon zest to a separate mixing bowl. Slowly whisk in the buttermilk mixture until thick and smooth. Next, fold the egg whites into the mix, one third at a time, until fully incorporated. Do not over mix; you want to keep as much air in the batter as possible.

Pour the cake batter into the prepared tin and bake for 45 minutes or until a skewer inserted into the centre of the cake comes out clean.

(continued on page 163)

Earl Grey & Lemon Drizzle Cake
(continued)

FOR THE EARL GREY SYRUP
50g (1¾ oz) caster sugar
Used tea leaves from
  buttermilk (see method)
70ml (5 tablespoons) water
30ml (2 tablespoons) lemon
  juice

FOR THE GLAZE
150g (5½ oz) icing sugar
8g (¹/₆oz) or 4 teaspoons of
  Earl Grey tea
1 teaspoon vanilla essence
Lemon zest, to decorate
  (optional)

While the cake is baking, make the Earl Grey syrup. Put the caster sugar, reserved tea leaves, water and lemon juice into a pan. Place over a medium heat and stir until the sugar has just dissolved and the mixture begins to bubble. Remove from the heat and set aside to cool.

When the cake is done, leave it in the tin for 15 minutes before pricking the top all over with a fork and drizzling evenly with the syrup. Leave the cake to cool completely in the tin before transferring it to a wire rack lined with a piece of baking paper or to a baking tray. (This will catch the drizzle.)

For the drizzle, brew the Earl Grey tea leaves in 100ml (3½fl oz) of just-boiled water for 5 minutes. Strain and add the Earl Grey tea to a mixing bowl with the vanilla. Little by little, whisk in the icing sugar until smooth then drizzle the glaze all over the top of the cake and let it drip down the sides. While it is still wet decorate with some lemon zest if you wish.

If you can resist, let the drizzle dry out for an hour or so before cutting the cake for eating.

Yunnan, Orange and Polenta Cake

This Chinese black tea has a caramel-cocoa flavour and a light smokiness when brewed. Here it is coupled with the bitter sweetness of oranges and the richness of butter and almonds. It goes without saying that this is perfect with a pot of freshly brewed Yunnan tea.

MAKES A 23CM (9 INCH) CAKE

200g (7oz) soft unsalted butter, plus extra for greasing

200g (7oz) caster sugar

200g (7oz) ground almonds

100g (3½ oz) fine polenta (cornmeal)

1½ teaspoons baking powder

4 medium eggs

Zest of 2 oranges (you will need the juice for the syrup)

FOR THE SYRUP

Juice of 2 oranges (about 125ml/4fl oz)

10g (¾ oz) or 5 teaspoons of Yunnan tea leaves

100g (3½ oz) caster sugar

This cake is perfect served with a dollop of crème fraîche or cream and more orange zest.

Preheat the oven to 180°C/350°F/Gas Mark 4 and grease and line a 23cm (9 inch) cake tin with baking paper.

Cream the butter and sugar together until light in colour and fluffy. Mix the almonds, polenta and baking powder in a separate bowl. Add this to the creamed butter and sugar and mix again to form a stiff batter. Add the eggs, one at a time, mixing well after each addition. Finally, beat in the orange zest.

Spoon the mixture into the prepared tin and bake in the oven for about 40 minutes until a caramel coloured crust has formed on top.

Meanwhile, make the syrup. Put the ingredients in a small saucepan over a medium heat. You can bring this to a simmer, stirring all the while, but once the sugar has dissolved and you have a clear liquid, turn off the heat and leave to steep for 10 minutes. Strain the liquid and set aside until the cake is cooked.

After 40 minutes, check the cake. It may seem soft to the touch at this point but if a skewer inserted into the centre of the cake comes out relatively clean, the cake is cooked. It wants to be light and only just cooked in order to be perfectly moist in the eating. Remove the cake from the oven, and leave it in its tin. Prick the top of the cake all over with a skewer and carefully pour the warm syrup over the surface, making sure it is evenly covered. Leave the cake in the tin for 15 minutes to let the syrup soak in before removing it and continuing to cool on a wire rack.

Assam Tea Cake

A quintessential teatime tea cake: rich, full-flavoured, just sweet enough to take the edge off the strength of the Assam and as comforting as a cup of perfectly milky tea. This recipe could happily be added to – chocolate chunks, chopped nuts or dried fruit are all possibilities – but there is something entirely pleasing about its simplicity: we would encourage you to try it just as it is (at least the first time).

MAKES A 900G (2LB) CAKE

12g or 6 teaspoons Assam tea leaves

180ml (6fl oz) whole milk

150g (5½ oz) unsalted butter, at room temperature, plus extra for greasing

100g (3½oz) caster sugar

2 medium eggs

80g (3oz) honey

½ teaspoon vanilla extract

250g (9oz) plain flour, plus extra for dusting

1½ teaspoons baking powder

½ teaspoon sea salt

Try soaking 200g your favourite dried fruit in brewed tea while you prepare your batter, then strain and stir the fruit into the mixture before baking. This will give an even richer tea flavour.

Preheat the oven on 350°F/175°C/ Gas Mark 3½ and line or grease and flour a 900g (2lb) loaf tin.

Place the tea leaves and milk in a saucepan over a medium heat and bring to a gentle simmer for 5 minutes. Take off the heat and leave to steep while cooling to room temperature. It should be the colour of strong milky tea. Strain the milk, discarding the tea leaves, and keep the infusion to one side.

Meanwhile, cream the butter and sugar together until light in colour and fluffy. Add the eggs, one at a time, and beat into the creamed butter. The mix may appear slightly curdled at this point. Don't worry – once the flour is added this minor wrong will soon be undone. Finally add the honey and vanilla extract and beat until combined.

In a separate bowl combine the flour, baking powder and salt. Beat the flour mixture into the creamed butter mixture, then add the milky tea and mix briefly to a smooth batter. Pour the batter into the lined loaf tin and bake for 50–60 minutes until the cake is golden-brown on top and a skewer inserted into the centre comes out clean.

Let the cake cool in the tin for 5 minutes before removing and cooling on a wire rack. This is delicious served still warm from the oven, but it can be at its best the following day, toasted and smeared with cold butter.

Spiced Ginger & Keemun Loaf Cake

This is a tea cake in surround sound. It is heady with nutmeg and ginger and warming with cinnamon and Keemun, a Chinese black tea that is both nutty and chocolatey in character. At the end of summer, when the changing season brings crisp orange leaves and early sunsets, this cake would make for a delicious mid-afternoon treat. You can't ask for much more than that.

MAKES A 900G (2LB) LOAF CAKE

- 75g (2½oz) black treacle
- 75g (2½oz) golden syrup
- 75g (2½oz) dark brown soft sugar
- 75g (2½oz) unsalted butter, plus extra for greasing
- 25g (1oz) Keemun tea leaves
- 75ml (2½fl oz) water
- 225g (8oz) plain flour, sifted, plus extra for dusting
- 1½ tablespoons ground ginger
- 2 teaspoons ground cinnamon
- ½ nutmeg, grated
- 2 medium eggs
- ½ teaspoon bicarbonate of soda
- 40ml (1½oz) milk

Preheat the oven to 170°C/340°F/Gas Mark 3½ and line or grease and flour a 900g (2lb) loaf tin.

Measure the black treacle, golden syrup, sugar, butter, tea leaves and water into a saucepan. Place over a medium heat and stir until the butter has melted and the mixture combined. Bring to a simmer, allow to bubble away for 3 minutes, then remove from the heat and set aside to cool.

Put the flour and spices into a large mixing bowl and add the syrup mixture, straining it through a sieve as you pour to remove the tea leaves, which you can discard. Stir the mixture well with a wooden spoon until smooth, then beat in the eggs, followed by the bicarbonate of soda and the milk.

Pour the batter into the prepared tin and bake for 60–70 minutes until well risen and firm. Remove the cake from the oven and allow to cool in the tin for 5 minutes before turning out onto a wire rack.

If you can bear to wait, store the cooled cake wrapped in its tin for 24 hours before eating – it will improve and intensify immeasurably. More likely, serve a few slices freshly baked and keep the rest of the cake for the following day, or the day after that, when it will be perfect spread with salted butter.

Iced Matcha & Lemon Loaf Cake

**MAKES A 900G (2LB)
LOAF CAKE**

170g (6oz) unsalted butter (room temperature), plus extra for greasing

170g (6oz) golden caster sugar

3 large eggs

170g plain flour, plus extra for dusting

3½ teaspoons baking powder

1½ tablespoons Matcha green tea powder, sifted

¼ teaspoon salt

Zest and juice of 1 lemon

1 tablespoon Greek yoghurt

FOR THE SYRUP

100g (3½ oz) caster sugar

50ml (2fl oz) water

Juice of 1 lemon

FOR THE ICING

50g (1¾ oz) unsalted butter, softened

25g (1oz) cream cheese, softened

200g (7oz) icing sugar, sifted

½ teaspoon Matcha green tea powder, sifted

1 tablespoon milk

¼ teaspoon vanilla essence

Light and fluffy, a little bitter, a little sweet, and luminous green from the Matcha, this cake is as striking as it is delicious, and always sells out first on the counter at our Tea Bar.

Preheat the oven to 170°C/340°F/Gas Mark 3 and line or grease and flour a 900g (2lb) loaf tin. Tap the tin edges on the work surface to remove excess flour.

Cream the butter and sugar together together with a stand mixer or hand-held mixer until light in colour and fluffy. Add the eggs, one at a time, mixing after each addition. Add the remaining dry ingredients and mix until just come together. Finally add the lemon zest and juice and the yoghurt and mix one last time.

Pour the cake batter into the prepared tin and bake in the middle of the oven for 45 minutes or until a skewer inserted into the centre of the cake comes out clean.

Meanwhile, make the syrup. Put the ingredients in a small saucepan, bring to the boil and simmer until dissolved.

Remove the cake from the oven and, leaving it in its tin, prick the surface all over with a fork before pouring over 4 tablespoons of the lemon sugar syrup. Let the cake cool for 20 minutes in its tin while you make the icing.

For the icing, cream the butter and cream cheese together until soft. Add the icing sugar a little at a time and mix well. Add the Matcha and ensure it is completely mixed in without any lumps. Finally, add the milk and vanilla and beat until bright green and fluffy. Spread the icing on the cooled cake and you are ready to slice and eat.

Niceties

Earl Grey & Cardamom Sugar Buns
by Dear Safia

We make no apology for dedicating another recipe to Earl Grey: this fragrant tea is a favourite for baking and for these delicious sugar buns, the endlessly talented British Iraqi baker Safia has paired it perfectly with the warm notes of cardamom.

MAKES 12

300ml (9fl oz) whole milk

6g or 3 teaspoons Earl Grey tea leaves

7g (1 sachet) fast-action dried yeast

75g (2½oz) butter, cubed and at room temperature

1 egg, plus extra for egg wash

100g (3½oz) caster sugar

500g (1lb 2oz) plain flour, plus extra for dusting

1 teaspoon salt

FOR THE EARL GREY & CARDAMOM FILLING

200g (7oz) granulated sugar

1.5g or ½ teaspoon Earl Grey tea leaves

1 teaspoon ground cardamom

100g (3½oz) unsalted butter, at room temperature

Preheat the oven to 170°C/340°F/Gas Mark 3.

Begin by infusing the milk for your dough. Put the milk and Earl Grey tea leaves in a saucepan and gently warm together until steaming. Remove from the heat and leave to steep until lukewarm.

Strain the warm, infused milk into the bowl of a stand mixer. Add the yeast and stir to dissolve, then add the butter in small cubes and stir until melted. Add the egg, sugar, flour and salt to the mixture. Using the dough hook mixer, mix at low speed until the dough comes together and begins to pull away from the side of the bowl. Don't overwork the dough as this will make the buns quite tough.

Shape the dough into a ball and place in a lightly oiled bowl. Cover with cling film and leave in a warm place to rise for 1 hour until almost doubled in size.

For the filling, put the sugar, tea leaves and ground cardamom in a food processor. Pulse for 2–3 minutes or until the tea leaves have broken down slightly and are well distributed throughout the sugar. Add 100g (3½oz) of this sugar mixture to the bowl of your stand mixer, add the butter and beat together until light in colour and fluffy. Set the remaining infused sugar aside.

(continued on page 172)

Earl Grey & Cardamom Sugar Buns
(continued)

Turn your risen dough out onto a clean, lightly floured surface and knead very briefly. Shape into a ball and roll out into a large rectangle roughly 40 x 20cm (16 x 8 inches). Spread the filling in a thin, even layer across the dough using a palette knife or the back of a spoon. Starting from one of the long edges of the rectangle, tightly roll the dough to form a thick log, like a Swiss roll. Then roll the dough back and forth on the surface using the palms of your hands to ensure it is an even thickness throughout.

Using a serrated knife, slice the dough into 12 equal rounds.

Butter a 12-hole muffin tray, sprinkle a little of your infused sugar over the butter, and place the rounds snugly into the holes. Cover with a tea towel and leave to rise for a further 30 minutes.

When risen, brush each bun with beaten egg and bake for 10–15 minutes, or until risen and golden brown. Be careful not to overbake them. Remove from the oven and carefully turn out the buns onto a wire rack. While the buns are still warm, dip each one into the remaining Earl Grey and cardamom sugar, ensuring they are completely covered.

These buns are best served the day they are made, and will likely all be eaten the minute they've had their sugar coating, but for any leftover you can always reheat them – they'll taste just as good the day after.

White Chocolate & Matcha Cookies

These cookies are both simple and delicious. Bright green from the Matcha and flecked with luxuriant white chocolate, they've got everything you want from a cookie, with the added intrigue and complexity that Matcha brings to the mix.

MAKES 24 COOKIES

150g (5½oz) salted butter, at room temperature

100g (3½oz) light brown sugar

50g (1¾oz) caster sugar

1 egg

240g (8½oz) plain flour

2 teaspoons Matcha green tea powder

½ teaspoon bicarbonate of soda

100g (3½oz) white chocolate chips

Preheat your oven to 170°C/340°F/Gas Mark 3 and line a baking sheet with baking paper.

Cream the butter and sugars together until they are light in colour and fluffy. Add the egg and beat well before stirring in the flour, Matcha powder and bicarbonate of soda. Do not overwork the dough – as soon as it has come together, stop. Add the white chocolate and mix a few more times to distribute.

Turn out the cookie dough onto a sheet of baking paper and use your hands to form the mix into a sausage about 5cm (2 inches) in diameter. Roll this up, twisting the ends like a Christmas cracker, and place in the freezer for at least 30 minutes.

To cook the cookies, slice a few 2cm (¾ inch) rounds from your chilled dough and place a few centimetres apart on the baking tray. If you want to cook the entire batch, use two baking trays. If you plan to only cook a few cookies, keep the rolled cookie dough in the freezer for next time. Transfer the baking tray(s) to the middle of the oven and cook for 12 minutes turning if necessary to ensure they cook evenly.

Remove from the oven and allow to cool on the tray. Do not be alarmed that the cookies look soft – they will continue to firm up as they cool and this is how we get that soft-centred-perfection that we are after.

Rooibos & Barley Fig Rolls
by Henrietta Inman

For Suffolk-based pastry chef and author of The Natural Baker,
Henrietta Inman, fig rolls are a childhood memory. Here she
teaches us to make our own from scratch, with the full body
and cherry notes of Rooibos tea complementing the rich
sweetness of the fig filling.

MAKES 20

FOR THE DOUGH

6g or 4 teaspoons Rooibos tea
leaves

80g (3oz) wholegrain barley
flour, plus extra for dusting

120g (4½oz) wholegrain spelt
flour

70g (2½oz) light brown
muscovado or coconut sugar

Pinch of sea salt flakes

Finely grated zest of 1 orange

100g (3½oz) virgin coconut
oil, melted

1 teaspoon vanilla extract

For the filling, add all the ingredients to a medium saucepan with 160ml (5½ fl oz) water and bring to the boil. Cook gently until the liquids are just absorbed. Remove from the heat and blend with a hand-held blender until relatively smooth. Set aside to cool.

For the dough, toast the tea leaves in a frying pan over a medium heat for 2 minutes, just enough to release the tea's flavours. Set aside to cool.

Mix the cooled tea leaves with the flours, sugar, salt and orange zest in a bowl. Add the coconut oil, 1 tablespoon of water and the vanilla extract and mix until well combined, bringing it together with your hands into a ball. Flatten the dough out on a lightly floured piece of baking paper to form a rough rectangle. Lightly flour the dough, place another piece of baking paper on top and roll it out to a 23 x 18cm (9 x 7 inch) rectangle. The dough should be a bit less than 5mm (¼ inch) thick. Remove the top sheet of baking paper.

FOR THE FIG FILLING

3g or 2 teaspoons Rooibos tea
   leaves
240g (8½oz) dried figs, stalks
   removed, roughly chopped
Finely grated zest and juice of
   1 orange
1 teaspoon vanilla extract
½ teaspoon ground cinnamon
15g (½oz) honey

Transfer the dough, still on the baking paper, to a baking tray. Form the cooled fig paste into a cylinder down the middle of the dough, leaving a rim of about 6cm (2½ inches) at the top and bottom edges. Carefully roll the bottom edge of the dough over the paste to meet the top edge, creating a cylinder shape with a flat bottom. Press along the joined edge to create a seal and then trim any excess dough off the edges. Refrigerate for 1 hour to firm up.

Preheat the oven to 180°C/350°F/Gas Mark 4. Line a baking tray with baking paper.

Cut the chilled dough into 1cm (½ inch) thick pieces using a sharp knife, and place on the prepared tray. Bake for 30 minutes, turning halfway so they colour evenly on both sides. Leave to cool slightly, then serve. These will keep for up to five days in an airtight container.

White Peony Madeleines

Madeleines are pot-bellied and scalloped little cakes from France. Once enjoyed warm from the oven with some rich crème fraîche it is hard to imagine a more delightful or provocative sweet treat. We've added to the indulgence with the honey and melon sweetness of our White Peony white tea. Not content with upgrading the madeleine itself, we've also steeped the crème fraîche in some Rooibos which, with its dried cherry and vanilla notes, takes this otherwise simple treat to a new level.

MAKES 12

135g (4½oz) unsalted butter, plus extra for greasing

2 tablespoons honey

4g or 2 tablespoons White Peony tea leaves

3 large eggs

30g (1oz) brown sugar

100g (3½oz) caster sugar

135g (4½oz) sifted plain flour, plus extra for dusting

FOR THE ROOIBOS CRÈME FRAÎCHE

100g (3½oz) crème fraîche

1 tablespoon Rooibos tea leaves

3 tablespoons water

You will need a madeleine tray for this recipe, ideally non-stick.

Preheat the oven to 200°C/400°F/Gas Mark 6.

Begin by melting the butter and honey in a small saucepan over a low heat. Once melted, add the tea leaves and simmer gently for 5 minutes, then set aside to cool.

Whisk the eggs and both sugars into a pale and frothy mixture. Fold in the flour, then add the cooled butter and honey mix, straining it through a sieve as you pour to remove the leaves, which you can discard. Stir the mixture and leave to rest for at least 3 hours.

Meanwhile, prepare your madeleine tray. Rub each mould liberally with butter, before scattering over a little flour in a fine layer.

Brew the Rooibos in 2 tablespoons of freshly boiled water for 4 minutes. Strain off the liquor and allow to cool. Fold this gently through the crème fraîche and set aside in the fridge until needed.

When ready to cook, spoon a heaped teaspoon of the cake batter into each mould in your prepared tray. Bake in the middle of the oven for 8–9 minutes. Remove when the madeleines are nicely risen and golden brown. Carefully flip the madeleines out of the tray using a small spoon. Serve immediately with a dusting of icing sugar and spoonful of the Rooibos crème fraîche. Delicious with fresh raspberries.

Ice Creams

Matcha Choc Ices

There is a ten-year-old you who will derive untold pleasure from these ridiculously simple choc ices. You will need silicone moulds to make these, which can easily be bought online or from any cook shop. Alternatively, if the shape doesn't worry you, you can use a large block ice cube tray or even a silicone muffin tray to get a similar effect.

MAKES 6-8 CHOC ICES

FOR THE CHOCOLATE
   COATING

200g (7oz) dark chocolate
   chips

200g (7oz) milk chocolate
   chips

FOR THE ICE CREAM

300ml (½ pint) double cream

200ml (7fl oz) condensed milk

150g (5½oz) Greek yoghurt

1 level teaspoon Matcha tea
   powder

Begin by melting the two chocolates together. Put the chocolate chips in a heatproof bowl set over a saucepan of simmering water, mix well to combine and, when melted, remove from the heat.

Next, coat your choc-ice moulds. Using a pastry brush, coat the base and sides of the moulds with a layer of chocolate roughly 2mm (¹/₁₆ inch) thick. Once coated, place in the freezer for at least 15 minutes while you make your ice cream. It is worth checking the moulds after 5 minutes as any gaps in the chocolate coating will be clearly visible. Patch these up with extra chocolate and return the moulds to the freezer until fully set. You should have at least a quarter of your melted chocolate left, so cover this in cling film and set aside.

The ice cream is very simple to make. Whisk all the ingredients, using either a stand mixer or hand-held mixer, until thick and voluminous. Remove the moulds from the freezer and spoon the ice-cream mixture into the lined moulds, using the edge of a spatula or a palette knife to give a smooth, level surface to the ice cream. Return them to the freezer for at least 3 hours, if not overnight, until solid.

(continued on page 182)

Matcha Choc Ices
(continued)

When frozen firm, re-melt the remaining chocolate for a few seconds in a microwave or over a pan of simmering water as before. Remove the choc ices from the freezer and brush the last layer of chocolate onto each one. You have to work quickly and decisively as the chocolate will harden almost immediately on contact with the ice cream. You'll find it easiest to work in layers until you have full coverage.

Return the choc ices to the freezer for a final 15 minutes to fully set the chocolate, before turning out and devouring. Once made, you can store these as they are in the freezer for several weeks. They will soften within a few minutes at room temperature. You may well want to serve them wrapped in a square of baking paper or alongside a big stack of napkins.

Rooibos & Vanilla Ice Cream

by Poco Gelato

Poco Gelato are a family-run business based in Southend-on-Sea, serving up some of the finest soft-scoop ice cream this side of Naples. After the success of the Good & Proper Tea X Poco Gelato collaboration in our Tea Bar one summer, we got the taste for tea ice cream and have shared a couple of their creations here for you to try at home. This recipe only really works in an ice cream machine.

SERVES 6

260ml (9fl oz) whole milk

140g (5oz) caster sugar

Pinch of salt

1 vanilla pod, halved
   lengthways and seeds
   scraped (reserve the pod)

35g (1¼ oz) wild Rooibos tea
   leaves

450ml (16fl oz) double cream

7 egg yolks

Put the milk, sugar, salt, vanilla seeds, tea leaves and half the cream into a heavy-bottomed saucepan and stir over a low heat. Turn off the heat before the mixture comes to the boil, cover with a lid and leave for 30 minutes to allow the flavours to infuse.

Pour the rest of the cream into a large bowl. Prepare an ice bath – the simplest way is to fill your sink with cold water and ice cubes.

In a separate bowl, whisk the egg yolks before pouring the warm milk and cream mix into the eggs, whisking. Return the mixture to the saucepan and set over a low heat, stirring, until it begins to thicken. Keep stirring, scraping the base and sides of the pan so that the mixture cooks evenly and the bottom doesn't scorch. Be patient and keep the heat low so that the mixture doesn't curdle.

Test the mixture by checking that it coats your spoon or spatula – as soon as it does, remove from the heat and slowly pour the mixture through a sieve into the bowl of cream. Place the reserved vanilla pod in the bowl and place over the ice bath. Stir the mixture until cool, then transfer the bowl to the fridge and chill for several hours.

When you're ready to churn, remove the vanilla pod and pour the chilled mixture into an ice-cream maker. Churn according to the manufacturer's instructions. Store in the freezer and enjoy.

Yunnan & Blood Orange Granita

The balance of sweet and sour from the blood orange and the rich, smoky flavour of the Yunnan tea makes this a very special granita.

SERVES 6

20g (1oz) or 10 teaspoons of Yunnan tea leaves

200g (7oz) caster sugar

Finely grated zest of 1 blood orange

500ml (18fl oz) blood orange juice (or, if you can't find any, use 400ml (14fl oz) orange juice and 100ml (3½ fl oz) grapefruit juice)

Begin by making your Yunnan tea. Measure out the tea leaves into a teapot or heatproof jug and steep it in 75ml (2½fl oz) of freshly boiled water for 4 minutes. Strain the tea, discarding the leaves, and set the liquor aside to cool while you make the rest of the granita mix.

Pour 200ml (7fl oz) of water into a saucepan and add the sugar. Place over a medium heat, swirling the pan to help the sugar dissolve but do not stir the mixture. Add the orange zest and the juice and bring to a simmer. Simmer gently for 5 minutes then remove from the heat and set aside to cool.

Stir in the tea liquor then pour the mixture into a shallow freezerproof container and place in the freezer. After 30 minutes, use a fork to rough up the mixture and distribute any ice crystals that are beginning to form. Do this three or four times, or every 30 minutes, during the freezing process, so that you ensure a smooth sorbet. The sorbet should be set after 2–3 hours.

To serve, simply rough up the surface of the sorbet with a fork and scrape the shards and shavings into little bowls or coupes.

Spiced Assam & Raisin Ice Cream
by Poco Gelato

Here is another yummy combination inspired by Poco Gelato's creations - this time a tea twist on a rum and raisin ice cream classic. This recipe only really works in an ice cream machine.

SERVES 6

25g (1oz) Assam tea leaves

75g (2½ oz) raisins

260ml (9fl oz) whole milk

140g (5oz) caster sugar

450ml (16fl oz) double cream

7 egg yolks

Scant ½ teaspoon ground cinnamon

¼ fresh nutmeg, grated

Scant ¼ teaspoon ground cloves

1 vanilla pod, halved lengthways and seeds scraped (reserve the pod)

Begin by brewing the Assam tea in 100ml (3½fl oz) freshly boiled water for 3 minutes. Strain the tea and pour the still-hot liquid over the raisins and leave to soak while you make your ice cream base.

Put the milk, sugar, spices, vanilla seeds and half the cream into a heavy-bottomed saucepan over a low heat. Gently warm while stirring. Turn off the heat before the mixture comes to the boil, cover with a lid and leave for 30 minutes to allow the flavours to infuse.

Pour the rest of the cream into a large bowl. Prepare an ice bath – the simplest way is to fill your sink with cold water and ice cubes.

In a separate bowl, whisk the egg yolks before adding the warm milk and cream mix and whisking briskly. Return the mixture to the saucepan and set over a low heat, stirring constantly until it begins to thicken. Keep stirring, scraping the base and sides of the pan so that the mixture cooks evenly and the bottom doesn't scorch. This bit takes a while: be patient and keep the heat low so that the mixture doesn't curdle.

Test the mixture by checking that it coats your spoon or spatula – as soon as it does, remove the pan from the heat and slowly pour the mixture through a sieve into the bowl of cream.

Place the reserved vanilla pod in the bowl and place over the ice bath. Stir the mixture until cool, then transfer the bowl to the fridge and chill for several hours.

When you're ready to churn, add the raisins together with the strong tea they were steeped in to the chilled mixture. Give everything a stir to distribute them evenly then pour into an ice-cream maker. Churn according to the manufacturer's instructions. Store in the freezer and enjoy.

Lemongrass, Lime & Ginger Sorbet

This is a lip-smackingly sharp sorbet. Perfect after rich or spicy food, especially on a hot summer evening.

SERVES 6

2.5cm (1 inch) piece of fresh root ginger, peeled and finely sliced

120g (4½oz) caster sugar

10g or 6 tablespoons of Lemongrass tea leaves

375ml (13fl oz) water

4 limes, 1 zested and all 4 juiced (you should get about 125ml (4fl oz) juice)

Put the ginger, sugar and Lemongrass tea in a saucepan with the water. Heat the pan, stirring regularly, until the sugar is fully dissolved and the air is heady with the scents of ginger and lemongrass. This should be about 5 minutes; the syrup doesn't need to boil. Remove the syrup from the heat, and allow to cool.

Once cool, whisk the lime juice and zest into the mixture. You want to do this when the syrup is cooler to keep the bright colour of the lime. Place the syrup in the fridge to cool fully – it will take about an hour at least. Strain the chilled syrup into a jug to remove the tea leaves and ginger pieces.

This sorbet works best made using an ice-cream machine. If you have one, pour the sorbet into the ice-cream maker and churn according to the manufacturer's instructions. If you don't have an ice-cream maker, pour the mixture into a shallow, freezer-proof container and place in the freezer. After 30 minutes, use a fork to rough up the mixture and distribute any ice crystals that are beginning to form. Do this three or four times, or every 30 minutes, during the freezing process, so that you ensure a smooth sorbet. The sorbet should be set after 2–3 hours. Store in the freezer.

To serve, use a warm spoon to scoop into little bowls or coupes.

187

Index

Acknowledgements

A publisher came to the van one rainy Tuesday back in 2013 and asked, over the counter, if I'd ever considered writing a book about tea. I hadn't, but naturally it sounded like an exciting thing to do. It occupied my thoughts for a few weeks, but after a series of emails back and forth, I didn't give it another thought until many years later. Those years passed by at terrifying speed, filled as they were with the day to day frenzy of running a business, and there was never a good moment to throw a book into the mix. The book is no doubt much the better for it, but there are a few people to thank for making it happen at last, not to mention the many more who have supported Good & Proper over the years. To Ben Benton for encouraging me to finally put pen to paper, and indeed putting his own pen to paper, too, to lighten the load. To Kyle Books for making it possible and bearing with my terrible timekeeping. To Steven Joyce for his beautiful photographs and inviting us into his light-filled, southeast London studio. To my parents for proofreading chunks of text sent late at night on WhatsApp, usually the night before a deadline. And, of course, to my husband Tom, for his unending support on every possible front, and for only once questioning my decision to write a book in the first mad months of motherhood...